Handy Reference

Differences between h... and desktop Windows

Action	Windows CE	
Open application	Double-tap on icon	Double-click on icon
Display shortcut menu	Tap while pressing Alt key	Right-click
Display information about the function of a button	Tap on button and hold down	Rest cursor over button
Minimise window	Tap on taskbar button	Click on Minimise button
Maximise window	Tap on taskbar button	Click on Maximise button
Switch between active applications	Press Alt+Tab, then select desired application from Task Manager	Press Alt+Tab
Summon Help	Tap on ?	Select appropriate heading from Help menu (or press F1)
Close dialog box and apply changes	Tap OK button	Click Apply and then later OK, or just OK button
Close dialog box without applying changes	Tap × button	Click Cancel button
Type in capitals only	Press both Shift keys at once	Press Caps Lock button
Create more storage space for files	Empty Recycle Bin *or* delete files/programs from storage memory *or* allocate more memory to storage	Empty Recycle Bin *or* delete files/programs from hard drive
Free system memory for applications	Close some active applications *or* allocate more memory to programs	Close some active applications

About the Series

In easy steps series is developed for time-sensitive people who want results fast. It is designed for quick, easy and effortless learning.

By using the best authors in the field, combined with our in-house expertise in computing, this series is ideal for all computer users. It explains the essentials simply, concisely and clearly - without the unnecessary verbal blurb. We strive to ensure that each book is technically superior, effective for easy learning and offers the best value.

Learn the essentials **in easy steps** - accept no substitutes!

Titles in the series include:

Operating Systems		Internet	
Windows 95	1-874029-28-8	CompuServe UK	1-874029-33-4
Windows CE	1-874029-80-6	FrontPage	1-874029-60-1
Applications – Integrated		HTML	1-874029-46-6
Microsoft Office 97	1-874029-66-0	Internet Explorer	1-874029-58-X
Microsoft Office	1-874029-37-7	Internet UK	1-874029-73-3
Microsoft Office SBE	1-874029-81-4	Netscape Navigator	1-874029-47-4
Microsoft Works	1-874029-41-5	**Accounting and Finance**	
SmartSuite (97)	1-874029-67-9	Microsoft Money UK	1-874029-61-X
Applications – General		Quicken UK	1-874029-71-7
Access	1-874029-78-4	Sage Instant Accounting	1-874029-44-X
Excel	1-874029-69-5	Sage Sterling for Windows	1-874029-79-2
PowerPoint	1-874029-63-6	**Graphics and Desktop Publishing**	
Word 97	1-874029-68-7	CorelDRAW	1-874029-72-5
Word	1-874029-39-3	PageMaker	1-874029-35-0
WordPerfect	1-874029-59-8	PagePlus	1-874029-49-0
Development Tools		Publisher	1-874029-77-6
Visual Basic	1-874029-74-1	**Hardware**	
Visual J++	1-874029-75-X	Upgrading Your PC	1-874029-76-8

For credit card sales and volume discounts Tel: 01926 817999 or EMail: sales@computerstep.com

For international orders and rights Fax: +44 1926 817005 or EMail: sevanti@computerstep.com

EMail your reader comments to: harshad@computerstep.com

Visit our web site at http://www.computerstep.com

WINDOWS CE
in easy steps

Leon Robbins

COMPUTER
STEP

In easy steps is an imprint of Computer Step
Southfield Road . Southam
Warwickshire CV33 OFB . England

Tel: 01926 817999 Fax: 01926 817005
http://www.computerstep.com

First published 1997

Notice of Liability

Every effort has been made to ensure that this book contains accurate
and current information. However, Computer Step and the author
shall not be liable for any loss or damage suffered by readers as a
result of any information contained herein.

Trademarks

Microsoft® and Windows® are registered trademarks of Microsoft
Corporation. All other trademarks are acknowledged as belonging to
their respective companies.

Acknowledgements

Computer Step would like to thank Compaq Computer Corporation
for use of their handheld PC.

Printed and bound in the United Kingdom

ISBN 1-874029-80-6

Contents

7 Customising Windows CE 101

8 Handheld/Desktop PC Communications 115

9 Internet Communications 131

Index 155

First Steps

This chapter explains how to set up your handheld PC the first time you use it, and then goes on to describe the components of the Windows CE screen. It explains how to get on-line help and how to check the battery level, finishing with a discussion of the potential for expanding Windows CE and the hardware on which it runs.

Chapter One

Covers

Introduction

Windows CE is Microsoft's new operating system for handheld PCs (also known as palmtops). These new computers, being developed by an ever-expanding number of manufacturers, allow you to carry around, in your pocket, a computer that runs a small, highly compacted operating system which will be very familiar to users of desktop versions of Windows. Most other handheld systems are very restricted in that they offer very little in the way of customisation and expandibility, in terms of hardware and software. Windows CE, however, allows much of the flexibility that has come to be expected of desktop Windows.

These similarities are not merely a superficial device intended to make Windows users feel at home; the two operating systems are in fact highly compatible. A Word document created on a desktop PC, for instance, can with the tap of a mouse be converted into a format that can be read by the Pocket Word application that is shipped with the Windows CE operating system; translation in the opposite direction is just as easy.

The upshot of this is that, using a handheld PC running Windows CE, you are no longer required to sit at a single desk in your office if you want to write a letter, use a spreadsheet or check your computerised address book; you can do all of these away from the desktop, and then exchange the data with your desktop PC whenever it is appropriate.

If you have bought a new Windows CE-oriented handheld PC, the operating system will have been pre-installed within the device. (Technical support will usually be provided by the manufacturers of the device, which include Casio, Compaq, Hewlett Packard, Hitachi, LG Goldstar, NEC and Philips.) In the rest of this chapter we will look at what happens when you start your machine for the first time, and then we will go on to examine the basic features of the new operating system.

Setting up your handheld PC

When you turn on your new handheld PC for the first time, you need to go through a simple setup procedure, to provide Windows CE with some information about yourself and your hardware. You need no technical knowledge to do this, and it should take less than five minutes to complete.

You should see the following screen:

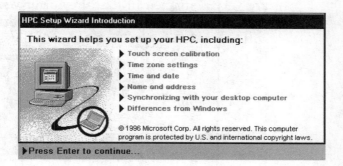

Calibrating the screen

1 Press the Enter key on the right-hand side of your keyboard to move to the next explanatory screen, then press Enter again. The following screen appears:

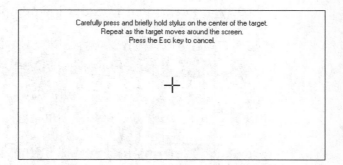

2 Take your handheld PC's stylus and tap it on the cross. Repeat this until you see a screen confirming that the new screen calibration settings have been measured.

3 Press Enter to move to the next screen...

Setting the time zone

The next stage asks you to provide some information about your geographical location.

4 Tap here. In the drop-down list, select the city that is the nearest to you.

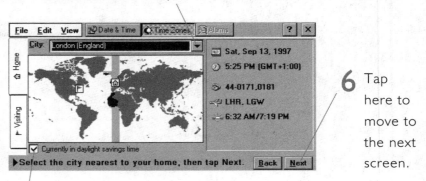

6 Tap here to move to the next screen.

5 Tap on this box to place a tick in it if your region is currently in daylight savings time.

Setting the date and time

Next, you need to enter today's date and time.

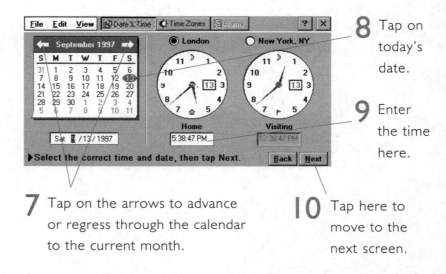

8 Tap on today's date.

9 Enter the time here.

7 Tap on the arrows to advance or regress through the calendar to the current month.

10 Tap here to move to the next screen.

Owner properties

This screen lets you enter personal details such as your name and address, so that your handheld PC can be returned to you if it is lost.

13 Tap here to enter any further notes.

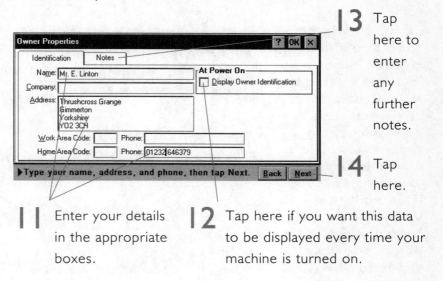

14 Tap here.

11 Enter your details in the appropriate boxes.

12 Tap here if you want this data to be displayed every time your machine is turned on.

Completing the setup process

The next few screens do not require any further input from you; they simply provide a little information about some features of Windows CE:

Tap Next when you've read each screen, then tap Done to complete the setup process.

The Windows CE screen

HANDY TIP

Users of desktop Windows will be familiar with the concept of "double-clicking": it usually involves resting the mouse cursor over an object, then quickly clicking twice with the left mouse button. In Windows CE, there is normally no visible cursor; to "double-click" on an object, use your stylus to tap twice on it in rapid succession.

HANDY TIP

Another technique that desktop Windows users will be acquainted with is "right-clicking" – clicking on an object with the right mouse button. To perform the corresponding action in Windows CE, press the Alt button and tap on the object.

The main screen of Windows CE is very similar to that of the desktop version of Windows, with which most PC users will be familiar. The main elements of the screen are pointed out below:

My Handheld PC. Double-tap here to view all the files on your handheld.

Recycle Bin. When you delete a file in Windows CE, it goes here first before being truly deleted. Double-tap here to view the bin's contents.

Program shortcut icons (superimposed with the ⬚ symbol). Double-tap to start a program.

Start button: tap on this to display a hierarchical menu of the programs and functions in Windows CE.

Battery level indicator

Clock

These elements are described in more detail in later chapters of the book. For how to start programs in Windows CE, see the following chapter: "Working with Programs".

Getting help

Most of the integral programs of Windows CE, and most other programs that you will install on it, come with a built-in on-line Help system. This provides concise, clear explanations of the major functions of each program, and should be your first resort to finding help, before diving for the manual. To activate Help about Windows CE itself, do the following:

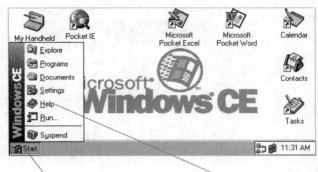

 HANDY TIP **If you see a question mark button in the top right-hand corner of an application's window, you can tap it to view that program's Help file.**

1 Tap once on the Start button.

2 Tap on Help in the Start menu.

3 A Help window appears. Tap on whichever of the underlined topics interests you. This will lead to other subtopics.

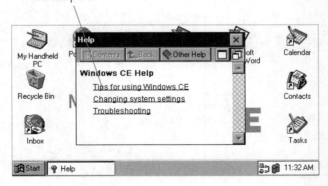

Eventually you should arrive at a Help document that is
relevant to your problem. Now do any of the following:

5 Tap here to see
   the main list of
   Help topics.

6 Tap here to expand the
   window to fill the whole
   screen (see step 9).

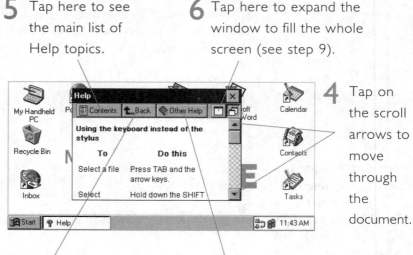

4 Tap on
   the scroll
   arrows to
   move
   through
   the
   document.

7 Tap here to
   move to the
   previous topic.

8 Tap here to see a list of the Help
   files for all the applications currently
   installed on your handheld PC.

9 Tap here to restore the window to its smaller size.

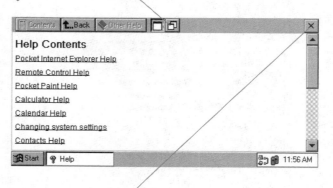

10 When you are finished, tap here to close the
   Help window.

Checking the battery level

BEWARE **If the "Very Low" heading is highlighted in bold, you should change your batteries immediately.**

Desktop PC users will not be used to worrying about the power source of their computer; a PC can be plugged into the mains, and left switched on all day, cheaply, and with little fear of there being a power-cut. However, your handheld PC is a different matter: it will run efficiently on batteries, but those batteries will discharge after several hours. Therefore, you should be mindful not to leave your handheld PC switched on when it is not being used, and you should monitor the charge level so that you are prepared when it is time to insert fresh batteries. Do the following to view information about your handheld's batteries:

2 Tap on the Power Off tab.

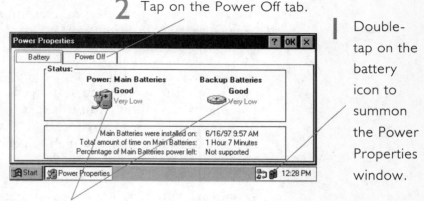

I Double-tap on the battery icon to summon the Power Properties window.

HANDY TIP **As an alternative to double-tapping on the battery icon, you can also display the Power Properties window by selecting Settings>Power from the Start menu.**

The main battery level and the backup battery level are shown here.

In order to conserve power, you can set your handheld PC to turn off if it is idle for a while, as follows:

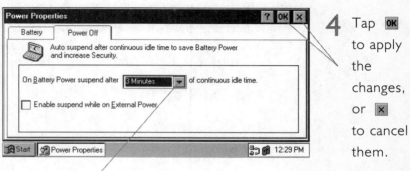

4 Tap **OK** to apply the changes, or **✕** to cancel them.

3 Tap here; select the idle power-off interval.

Expanding the handheld's capabilities

Like the desktop version of Windows, Windows CE – and the hardware it runs on – are extremely flexible in terms of the ways in which they can be enhanced and customised. The first way in which you are likely to make an addition to your handheld is to install some new software – see the section "Downloading from the Internet" in the following chapter.

A wide range of hardware add-ons are also available, using compact "PC cards", which fit everything into a small card that slots into a port on your handheld PC. A credit card-sized modem card, for example, allows your handheld to connect to the Internet (if you have an account with an Internet service provider) and communicate via email or browse the World Wide Web.

You can also buy pager cards, which allow you to receive textual messages without being connected to the telephone system via a modem. One step up from this is the wireless modem, which allows you to use a full email system and browse the web from any location. Many other types of card are also available, for a range of specialised purposes. However, if you find that there is no handheld PC card available for the purpose you require, you can purchase a serial card which will allow you to connect any serial device to the handheld: modems, digital cameras, bar-code readers, etc.

One small problem with using PC cards, however, is that they are notoriously power-hungry: they can drastically reduce the already-short lifespan of your handheld's batteries. While many PC card and serial devices come with their own power supplies (e.g. separate battery packs), it is still normally the best policy to use an external mains power supply when using any extra hardware with your handheld PC.

Working with Programs

This chapter helps you get to grips with the basic techniques that you will use to operate Windows CE. You will see how to start a program, how to handle program windows, and how to download programs from the Internet. Finally, you will learn how to remove programs that have been installed on your handheld PC.

Covers

Chapter Two

Starting programs

Before you can do anything really useful in Windows CE, you need to run a program (such as a word-processor or spreadsheet), which you use to enter, read or edit information. There are several possible ways to start a program in Windows CE, of which some or all may be appropriate.

REMEMBER

Many programs will also have shortcut icons directly on the main screen; double-tap on any of these to start the program automatically.

Most programs which have been properly installed on your handheld PC will have an entry on the Start menu. This is the menu that pops up when you tap on the Start button in the bottom left-hand corner of the Windows CE screen.

HANDY TIP

If you know a program is installed on your handheld PC, but you can't find a Start menu entry or shortcut for it anywhere, you can look for the program file itself. See the following chapter for how to use Windows CE Explorer to do this.

1 Tap here.   **2** In the Start menu, tap on "Programs".

This displays a view of the \Windows\Programs folder on your handheld PC. Within this folder you will see two types of icons: program shortcuts, and further folders.

3 Tap on a sub-folder to open it; or...

4 Tap on a shortcut icon to open its target program.

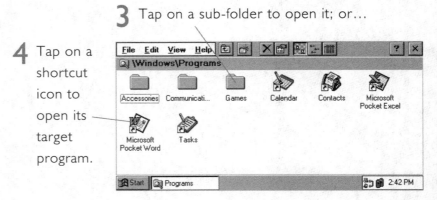

Exploring a typical program window

Almost any program window that you will see in Windows CE will have certain basic elements that are common to all other program windows. These include buttons, scrollbars, drop-down lists and menus.

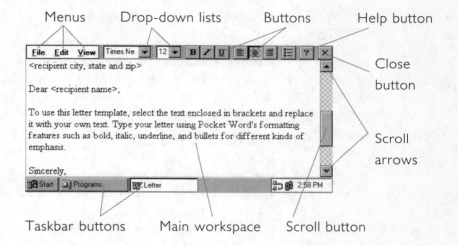

Menus   Drop-down lists   Buttons   Help button

Close button

Scroll arrows

Taskbar buttons   Main workspace   Scroll button

Menus

Tap on a menu heading to reveal a list of actions pertaining to functions that can be performed by the program. From this list, select any entry to move to the appropriate dialog box. The menus seen in the example above (File, Edit, View) are common to most Windows CE programs. Many menu functions can also be accessed by tapping on specialised buttons.

Buttons

These allow the user to toggle between values of a specific parameter, such as whether or not some word-processor text is underlined.

Drop-down lists

These allow the user to change variables with a wide potential range of values, without using a special dialog box. For example, the two drop-down lists shown above are used to change the font and font size of word-processor text. To see the list's range of possible values, tap on the button to its right: ■, then choose an option.

Scroll button

If a document, list or some other window item is too large to fit within the space allocated for it, scrollbars will appear along its vertical and/or horizontal axes, to allow you to view the whole of its contents. Tap on the button in a scrollbar with your stylus, then drag it in the direction of the area you want to reveal.

Scroll arrows

As an alternative to dragging the scroll button, you can tap on the arrows at either end of a scrollbar to adjust the viewing area bit-by-bit.

Taskbar buttons

These appear in the Windows CE taskbar, not in the program window, but are a function of programs. For each window that is open at any time, a button appears on the taskbar; when the window is closed, its button disappears from the taskbar. Taskbar buttons are used to minimise and maximise windows, as we will see in the following topic.

Close button

Used to shut down a window – see the following topic.

Help button

Used to open a program's Help file (if available). The Help button will not be present in the windows of programs with no Help file. For a closer look at Help files, see the topic "Getting help" in Chapter One.

Working with windows

The desktop version of Windows allows most program windows to exist in any one of three states: a window can be maximised, minimised, or in an intermediate state. In the latter state, the dimensions of the window can usually be adjusted by the user. However, owing to the relative smallness of the handheld PC's screen, the intermediate state is usually not available in Windows CE; only a small amount of information can be seen in the maximised view, so an intermediate state would be of little use.

When you first run a program, it is usually displayed in the maximised state:

REMEMBER

The only program in the main Windows CE package that allows a window to exist in the intermediate state is the Help interface, which provides two buttons for the purpose:

Restore

Maximise ———

This is particularly helpful in that it allows you to view a program and its Help screen alongside each other.

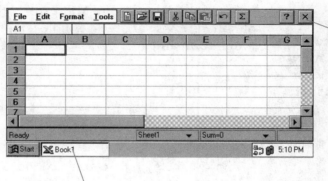

3 To close the window, tap here.

| To minimise the window, tap on its taskbar button...

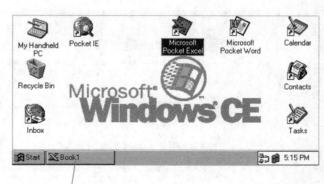

2 To maximise the window again, tap once more on the taskbar button.

Downloading from the Internet

One of the beauties of Windows CE over other handheld computer operating systems is that it is very easy to install new software. You don't need to plug a new card or chip into an expansion slot; in fact, it is almost as easy as installing new software on your desktop PC. The main difference is that you perform the installation not from the handheld, but from the desktop. This means that the more powerful computer performs most of the number-crunching involved in expanding the compressed installation files, and no redundant files are left lying around on your storage-hungry handheld.

One of the best places to start looking for Windows CE software to download is Microsoft's own web site. A range of software is available here, developed by Microsoft and other companies.

HANDY TIP

For more on Windows CE, including information on any new developments, access a higher level of the Microsoft web site:

`http://www.`
`microsoft.com/`
`windowsce`

1 On your desktop PC, establish an Internet connection and open the following address in your web browser:

`http://www.microsoft.com/windowsce/hpc/software`

2 Follow the hyperlinks to a download area that interests you, then click on the download link. When you are prompted to specify where to save the file, save it to the desktop.

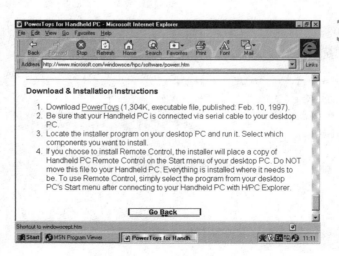

3 When the download is finished, disconnect from the Internet.

...contd

For how to connect your handheld PC to your desktop PC using the serial cable and HPC Explorer, see Chapter Eight.

4 Connect your handheld PC to your desktop PC via the serial cable.

5 Locate the file that you have just downloaded on the desktop and double-click on its icon.

After step 5, all the following procedures will be determined by the software you have just downloaded. The installation of one piece of software is shown below to give you an idea of the sort of process involved.

6 Proceed through the introductory screens by clicking on Next.

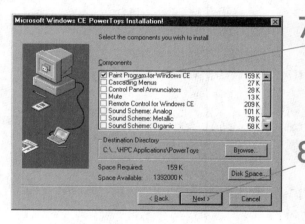

7 Click on the boxes to select only those components you wish to install.

8 Click Next, and then Finish to complete the installation.

The files are copied to the handheld.

9 An icon is added for each program installed. Double-tap it to open the program.

2 Working with Programs   **23**

Uninstalling programs

HANDY TIP

For more on the subject of allocating storage and program memory, see the topic "Changing memory allocation" in Chapter Seven.

Once you begin to install new programs on your handheld PC, you will soon come to realise the limitations of its memory capacity. As you use up the storage memory, the program memory is eaten away, meaning that you will be able to run fewer programs at any one time. The solution to this is to uninstall one or more of the programs that you have added. This is a very easy process:

1 Tap the Start button, then select Settings to show the Control Panel.

2 Double-tap on the Remove Programs icon.

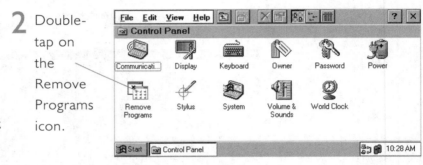

REMEMBER

You will notice that not all the programs that you have on your handheld PC are listed in the Programs list. This is because some of them, such as Pocket Word, Pocket Excel, the Information Manager, etc., are integral to the Windows CE operating system, and are stored in the handheld's ROM, which is unalterable.

3 The Remove Program Properties window appears, with a list of the programs that you can remove. Tap on the name of the program you want to delete.

4 Tap here.

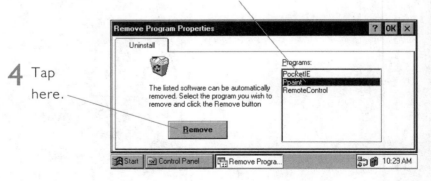

5 You will be asked to confirm that you want to uninstall the program. Tap Yes to complete the removal process.

Managing Files and Folders

This chapter deals with managing files and folders, which are the building blocks of Windows CE and of all the programs and documents you will use with it. Most file and folder management is performed with the Windows CE Explorer program, which will be the focus of the following pages.

Covers

Chapter Three

The Explorer window

Once you have learnt how to run programs in Windows CE, you will need to deal with the concept of files and folders. These are central to the day-to-day functioning of your handheld PC. Whenever you create a word-processor document, or edit a spreadsheet, you are creating or changing files. There are hundreds of files even on your handheld PC. They are organised into folders, which act as containers and organisational aids. Windows CE comes with a program known as Explorer, which you can use to move files from one folder location to another, and to perform other related operations.

To open the Explorer window, do the following:

HANDY TIP

There is an alternative way of starting Explorer: simply double-tap on the My Handheld PC icon.

2 Tap here.

1 Tap on the Start button.

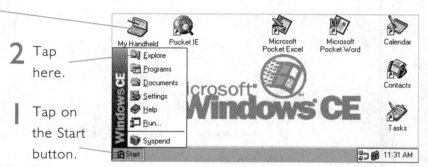

The Explorer window appears:

REMEMBER

Some folders are labelled with special icons: these are system folders which are related to specific elements of the Windows CE operating system, and should not be deleted.

File, Edit, View and Help menus

Icon bar

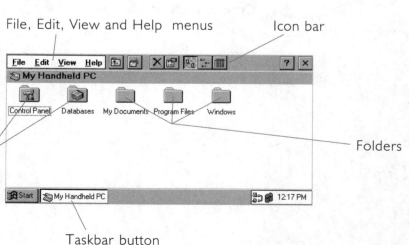

Folders

Taskbar button

The Explorer icon bar

The icon bar at the top of the Explorer window provides icons which you can tap on to perform commonly-used file operations. To use Explorer effectively, you should learn their functions:

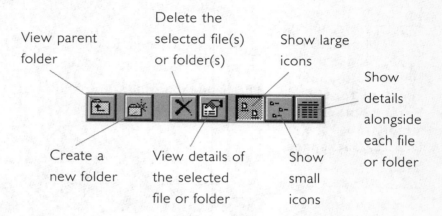

View parent folder

Delete the selected file(s) or folder(s)

Show large icons

Show details alongside each file or folder

Create a new folder

View details of the selected file or folder

Show small icons

Navigating through folders

You should think of the structure of folders and files stored on your handheld PC as a sort of inverted tree, with a single node at the top level, and many nodes at the bottom level.

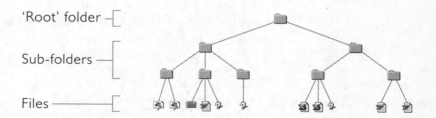

'Root' folder

Sub-folders

Files

Any folder may contain any number of sub-folders and/or any number of files. The folder one step up the hierarchy from any particular folder is known as its 'parent' folder. The only folder on your handheld PC that does not have a

...contd

parent folder is the one at the very top of the hierarchy – the 'root' folder. In Windows CE, this folder has the name 'Desktop'. Let us look at its contents:

1 Open the Explorer window as shown on page 26. The directory shown is 'My Handheld PC'.

If you prefer to use a keyboard shortcut for the Parent Folder icon, simply press the Delete/Backspace key.

2 Tap on the Parent Folder icon.

The Explorer window now shows the contents of the parent folder, 'Desktop'.

The Parent Folder icon is now dimmed, since this is the root folder, at the top of the folder hierarchy.

Note that these icons echo exactly the icons that you see on your Windows CE main screen; in effect, this is just another view of the same group of files. Double-tapping on any of them will have just the same effect as if you were double-tapping on their counterparts on the main screen.

To navigate in the opposite direction – i.e., to view the contents of a folder – double-tap on the folder.

Creating new folders

You are by no means restricted to using the folders that are already present in Windows CE; you can add as many as you like, in accordance with your own organisational requirements. For example, if you are at work on a project for which you have created a number of Word documents (see Chapter Four), you can group them all together in their own special folder. They will then be much easier to find than if they were mixed up with many other, unrelated files.

To create a folder, do the following:

1 Navigate to the folder within which you wish to create the new folder, using the techniques discussed on the previous pages.

2 Tap on File, then New Folder.

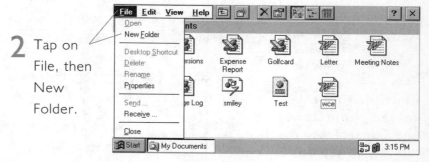

The new folder appears, with a dummy title beneath it:

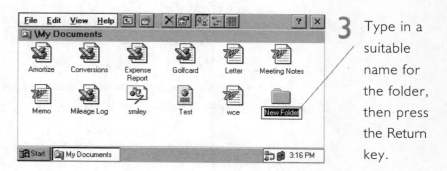

3 Type in a suitable name for the folder, then press the Return key.

Double-tap on the new folder to open it.

Copying and moving files

Once the structure of your folders is in satisfactory order, you may want to reorganise the files within them. How you should go about this depends on the source and destination folders.

Dragging file icons

In the desktop version of Windows, the easiest way to move or copy files is to drag them from one folder view to another. If you want to drag a file from one directory into an immediate subdirectory, this is also the easiest way in Windows CE. Do the following:

You can use exactly the same technique to move or copy folders.

Re step 1 – if you want to move or copy multiple files or folders, hold down the Control key while you tap on each icon in succession.

3 Without removing the stylus from the screen, drag the file onto the folder's icon.

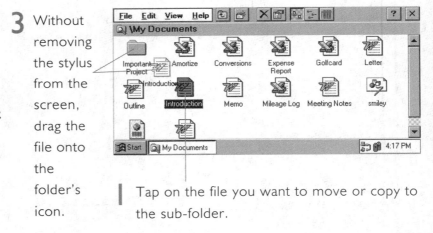

Tap on the file you want to move or copy to the sub-folder.

2 If you want to copy the folder rather than move it, hold down the Control (or 'CTRL') key now, and don't let go until you have completed step 4.

4 Lift the stylus from the screen when the file's icon is in place. The file is moved or copied to the new folder.

Using Cut, Copy and Paste

If you wish to move or copy files or folders to a location other than a direct sub-folder of their current folder, you can't use the tap-and-drag method, since the destination folder will not be visible when the source folder is being viewed. This is not a problem in the desktop version of Windows, since that gives you two separate panes in which to view the contents of your PC, one for folders and one for files. Also, the Explorer window in Windows CE must be either minimised or maximised; it cannot exist in an intermediate state. Therefore, it is not possible to open two separate instances of Explorer, each showing the contents of different folders, and drag files from one window to the other.

Instead, you must use the Cut, Copy and Paste commands (which are also present in the desktop version of Windows). These use the familiar clipboard system: you copy or cut files/folders to the clipboard, navigate to the correct folder, and then paste the contents of the clipboard. This is shown below:

1 In the source folder, select the file(s)/folder(s) you wish to move or copy. (See the Handy Tip on the previous page.)

2 Tap Edit.

3 To move the selected items, tap Cut; to copy them, tap Copy.

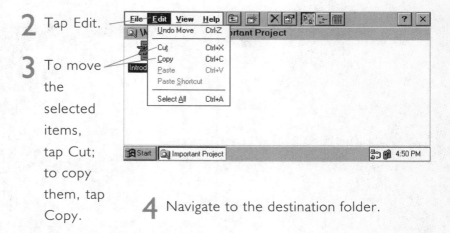

4 Navigate to the destination folder.

5 In the
target
folder,
tap Edit.

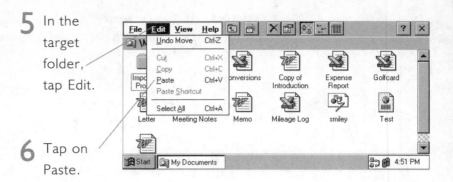

6 Tap on
Paste.

The contents of the clipboard are then pasted into the destination folder. If you selected the Cut command in step 3, you will find that the files or folders have now been deleted from their original location.

Deleting files

Deleting files or folders is a very easy task, but should be done with care: you could have a big problem on your hands if you delete the wrong items. Do the following:

1 Select the file(s) or folder(s) you want to delete.

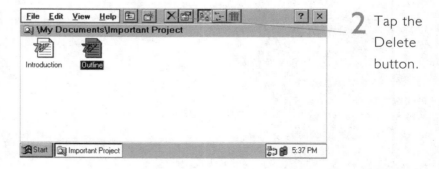

2 Tap the
Delete
button.

3 In the dialog box that follows, tap Yes to affirm that you do want to perform the delete operation. The selected objects are then sent to the Recycle Bin (see the following page).

The Recycle Bin

When you tell Windows CE to delete files from your handheld PC, they are not actually removed straight away, but are sent to the Recycle Bin. This is a safety feature which means that if you subsequently decide that you didn't really want to delete the files, they haven't yet been lost for good.

The Recycle Bin's icon is always present on your handheld PC's main screen. Double-tap on it to reveal its contents.

Recycle Bin

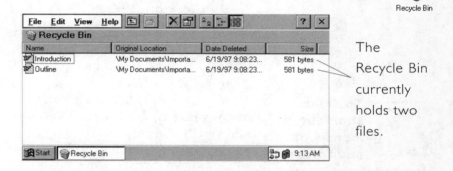

The Recycle Bin currently holds two files.

You can do either of two things to the files in the Recycle Bin: delete them, or restore them to their original locations. Follow steps 1 and 2 below, then either step 3, 4 or 5:

REMEMBER

Re step 1: to select multiple files, press the Control key while tapping on successive icons. Alternatively, to select a range of contiguous files, tap on the first in the range, then hold down the Shift key while tapping on the last.

1 Select the files you want to affect.

2 Tap on File in the menu bar.

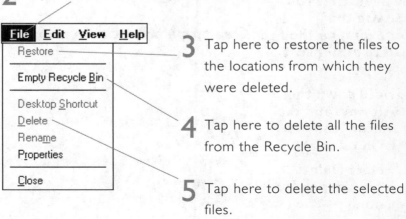

3 Tap here to restore the files to the locations from which they were deleted.

4 Tap here to delete all the files from the Recycle Bin.

5 Tap here to delete the selected files.

Creating shortcut icons

A typical shortcut icon

Microsoft Pocket Word

The files on your handheld PC that you will be most concerned with are program files and the document files that you create using those programs. Every file is stored in a particular folder; to open a document or run a program, you can navigate to it in Explorer, and then double-tap on its icon. However, many files are located at the bottom of a complicated tangle of directories, and it would be tiresome to have to navigate through these every time you want to open a commonly-used file. Hence, a quicker way is needed of opening popular files.

Shortcut icons, superimposed with the ⊡ symbol, provide the answer: they contain no real program or document information themselves, but act as pointers to other files. You can create as many shortcut icons as you want for any document or program, in whatever locations you feel to be most convenient. All shortcuts are essentially the same, but Windows CE allows you to create them in two different ways, depending on where you want to put them: on the main screen, or in any other folder.

HANDY TIP

To delete shortcut icons from any folder, you can if you want use the method described in "Deleting files" on page 32. However, to delete files on the main screen, this option will not be available. You can use the following method to delete either sort of file:

1. Hold down the Alt key, and tap on the icon you wish to delete.

2. Select Delete from the pop-up menu.

Creating a shortcut on the main screen

1 Use Explorer to navigate to the file for which you wish to create a shortcut, and select it.

2 Open the File menu, and choose Desktop Shortcut.

Creating a shortcut in any other folder

1 Use Explorer to navigate to the file for which you wish to create a shortcut, and select it.

2 Open the Edit menu, and choose Copy.

3 Navigate to the folder in which you wish to place the shortcut.

4 Open the Edit menu, and choose Paste Shortcut.

Pocket Word

Probably the most common task for which you will use your handheld PC is the creation of word-processor documents using Pocket Word, the miniature version of Microsoft Word, which comes with every handheld PC running Windows CE. As might be expected, it does not have such a huge range of features as its desktop counterpart, but Pocket Word is still a remarkably effective little program which will become indispensable in your day-to-day use of the handheld.

Covers

Overview

Most users of Pocket Word will already be acquainted with the desktop PC version of Word, and will want to use the Pocket version to create basic documents away from their desktop PC, and then upload them to the desktop for fine-tuning and printing. This is the intended use of Pocket Word. It provides many more functions than a simple text editor, such as Notepad for desktop PCs, but will not allow you to perform such niceties as using coloured text, adding frames or running a spell-check. However, Pocket Word does allow you to:

- Create documents using many different fonts

- Apply different font sizes

- Make text bold, italic or underlined

- Align text to the left, the centre or the right of the page

- Apply bullets to selected paragraphs

- Rearrange text using the clipboard

- Find and replace selected text

- View your documents in Normal or Outline view

All of these features will be covered in this chapter, and we will conclude by looking at how to exchange files between Pocket Word and the desktop PC version.

Opening Pocket Word

HANDY TIP

If the shortcut icon for Pocket Word has been deleted from your main screen, tap the Start button, then select Programs and double-tap on the Microsoft Pocket Word icon.

To open Pocket Word, make sure the Windows CE main screen is visible, and do the following:

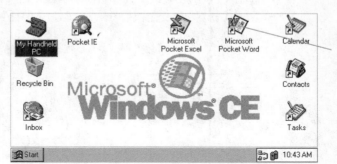

Double-tap here.

REMEMBER

Users of the desktop version of Word will be used to having several Word documents open at the same time, each document having a separate window within the main Word window. In Pocket Word, you can have as many documents open as memory allows, but they appear as separate instances of the Pocket Word program, each with its own button on the main Windows CE taskbar.

The Pocket Word window opens, with a blank document space ready for you to start typing. The main components of the Window are outlined below:

File, Edit and View menus

Font drop-down list

Font size drop-down list

Bold, italic & underline buttons

Paragraph alignment buttons

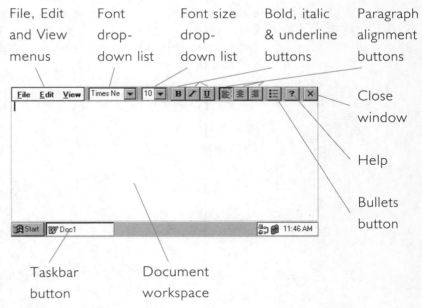

Close window

Help

Bullets button

Taskbar button

Document workspace

Entering text

The first thing you will want to do once you have opened Pocket Word is to begin entering text. As you do this, you will need to know how to navigate around the window. Begin by entering some text using the keyboard:

Text cursor

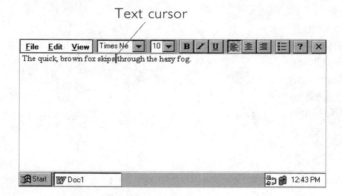

All text is entered using the cursor; as you type in text, the cursor moves so that it is always at the right of the last character you typed. To move the cursor so that you can change the text anywhere else in the document, use the following techniques:

1 To move the text cursor to any point in the text, use the cursor keys, or tap the area with the stylus.

2 To move the text cursor to the beginning of the current line, press the Alt key and then the left cursor arrow key.

3 To move the text cursor to the end of the current line, press the Alt key and then the right cursor arrow key.

4 To move through the text word-by-word rather than character-by-character, press the Control key as you use the cursor keys.

5 To move to the start or end of the document, press Alt and then the up or down cursor arrow keys.

Selecting text

If you want to change the properties of text that you have already typed, you need first to select it. There are several ways of doing this. The easiest is to use the stylus:

HANDY TIP

If you prefer to select text character-by-character without using the stylus, hold down the Shift key where you want the selection to begin, then expand the selection area using the cursor keys.

1 Press the stylus on the screen at the point where you wish the selection to begin.

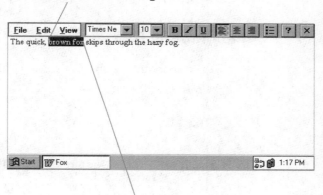

2 Drag the stylus across the text, without removing its tip from the screen, until all of the required text is selected.

If you want to select specific units of text automatically, do any of the following:

1 To select a whole word without dragging the stylus over it as above, simply double-tap on it.

2 To select a whole paragraph, triple-tap on any part of it.

3 To select a whole document, choose "Select All" from the Edit menu.

Changing character properties

A number of character properties can be changed, including the font, the font size and the font style (whether it is bold, italic or underlined). If you change any of these properties before selecting any text, then all text entered subsequently at the cursor will have the new properties. On the other hand, if you do select some text, only that text will acquire the new properties.

Changing the font

1 If you only want to change some of the text in the document, select it.

2 Tap here.

3 Select a font from the list, using the arrow buttons to scroll through it.

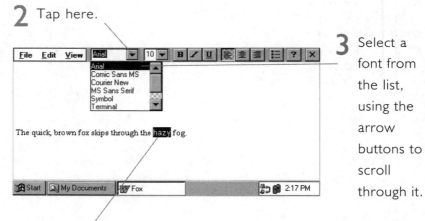

4 The font is changed. Be sure to deselect the text (by tapping anywhere on the screen) before continuing to type, unless you want the selected text to be replaced.

...contd

HANDY TIP

For an explanation of how to add fonts to your handheld PC, see "Installing extra fonts" in Chapter Seven.

Changing the font size

The range of font sizes available in Pocket Word is not as large as in the desktop version of Word, but those that are available are perfectly adequate for most simple purposes, such as creating headings or block quotes of smaller text.

1 If you only want to change some of the text in the document, select it.

2 Tap here.

| File Edit View Times Ne ▼ 18 ▼ B / U ≡ ≡ ≡ ≔ ? X |
| 8 |
| 10 |
| 12 |
| 14 |
| 18 |
| 22 |

The quick, brown fox skips through the hazy fog.

Start | My Documents | Fox | 2:28 PM

3 Select a font size from the list.

4 The font size is changed. Deselect the text (by tapping anywhere on the screen) before continuing to type, unless you want the selected text to be replaced.

Changing the font style

Pocket Word lets you make text bold, italic, underlined, or a combination of any of the three. This is achieved using the three font style buttons. If the text under the cursor has any of these styles applied to it, the appropriate button appears to be depressed.

1 If you only want to change some of the text in the document, select it.

2 Tap here to make the text bold

3 Tap here to make the text italic.

4 Tap here to make the text underlined.

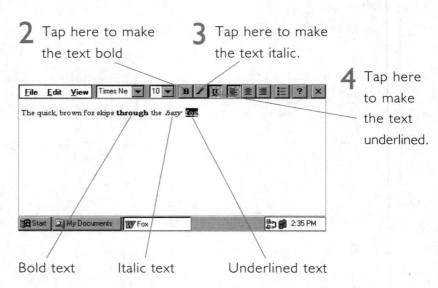

Bold text   Italic text   Underlined text

Changing paragraph properties

While the character properties discussed on the preceding pages can be applied to any number of characters (from a single letter up to the whole document), paragraph properties must be applied to a whole paragraph or a number of paragraphs. These features include text alignment and bulleted paragraphs.

REMEMBER

Since text-alignment changes apply to a whole paragraph, you can just tap inside a paragraph at step 1 if that is the only paragraph you wish to change; you don't have to select any of the text.

Changing text alignment

1 Select the paragraph(s) whose alignment you want to change.

2 Tap on the appropriate alignment button:

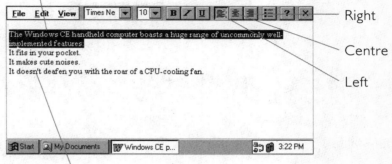

Right

Centre

Left

All of these paragraphs are currently left-aligned.

This paragraph has been centre-aligned.

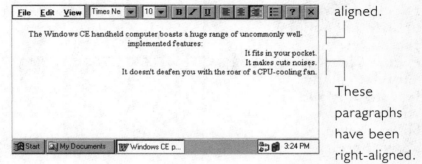

These paragraphs have been right-aligned.

Applying bullets to paragraphs

If you have a list of points which you would like to highlight individually in your document, you might like to bullet them: this indents the left edge of paragraph, and places a large dot at the beginning of the first line.

Each of the points you want to highlight must be on a separate line, in a different paragraph.

1 Tap in the paragraph you wish to apply a bullet to, or select a range of paragraphs.

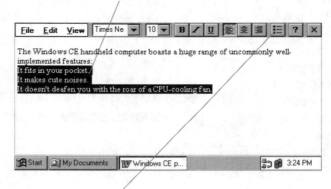

2 Tap the Bullets icon.

The selected paragraphs have been bulleted:

Most word-processor applications for desktop PCs allow the user to select from a range of different bullet characters. In Pocket Word, the automatic bullet feature only allows you to use the bullet symbol shown here.

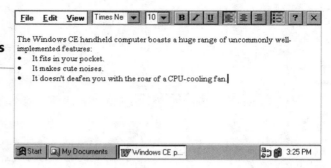

Using the clipboard

Pocket Word allows you to duplicate and move text within or between documents, using the clipboard. To use this, do the following:

HANDY TIP

As an alternative to using the Edit menu to access the clipboard, you can use the following keyboard shortcuts to speed things up:

Cut   Control + X
Copy   Control + C
Paste   Control + V

1 Select the text you want to duplicate or move.

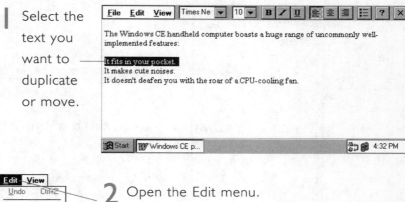

2 Open the Edit menu.

3 If you want to duplicate the selected text, choose Copy; if you want to move it (as in this example), choose Cut.

The selected text now exists on the clipboard.

4 Place the cursor where you intend to paste the contents of the clipboard.

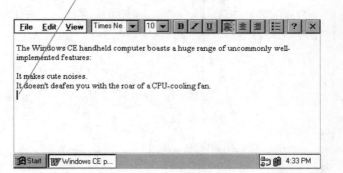

5 Open the Edit menu and choose Paste.

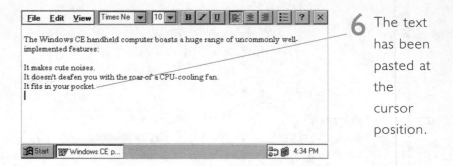

6 The text has been pasted at the cursor position.

Exchanging data with other documents

When using the clipboard in Pocket Word, you are not restricted to moving data around within a single document: if you have two documents open (see the Remember tip on page 37), you can copy or cut text from one document and paste it into the other.

Furthermore, you can use the clipboard to exchange data with other programs on your handheld PC. For example, if you have some text in Pocket Word which you wish to place in a Pocket Excel spreadsheet (see the next chapter), simply copy the text onto the clipboard. Now minimise the Pocket Word window and open or maximise Pocket Excel. Select the cell into which you wish to paste the text, then select Copy from the Edit menu: the text is pasted directly into the cell.

You may also find it very helpful to use the same procedure to exchange text between Pocket Word and Inbox, Windows CE's email program

Finding and replacing text

If you need to locate a piece of text in a document which you know is there, but you cannot find it, the Find function will locate it in a split-second. Likewise, if you need to replace a commonly-occurring word or phrase with another, the Replace function will do this automatically.

Finding text

To locate a particular word or phrase in a document, do the following:

1 Open the Edit menu and select Find.

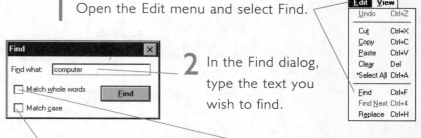

2 In the Find dialog, type the text you wish to find.

If you prefer, you can use keyboard shortcuts instead of the Edit menu to perform Find operations:

Find   Control + F
Find Next   Control + 4

4 If you only wish your search to find text that constitutes whole words (e.g., in this case, if you don't want it to flag words such as "computers" or "computerisation"), check this box.

3 If you only wish to find text matching the case of the text you entered, check this box.

5 Tap the Find button.

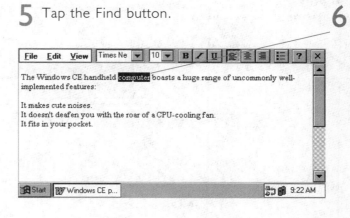

6 The first instance of the search text is highlighted. To find the next, select Find Next from the Edit menu.

Replacing text

The Replace dialog is basically the same as the Find dialog, except it provides an extra box in which you can enter text with which to replace the found text.

Select Replace from the Edit menu.

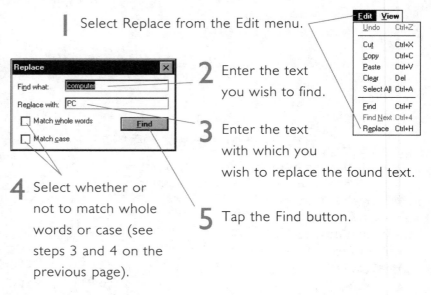

2 Enter the text you wish to find.

3 Enter the text with which you wish to replace the found text.

4 Select whether or not to match whole words or case (see steps 3 and 4 on the previous page).

5 Tap the Find button.

HANDY TIP

If you prefer, you can use keyboard shortcuts instead of the Edit menu to perform Find and Replace operations:

Find	Control + F
Find Next	Control + 4
Replace	Control + H

The first instance of the search text is highlighted. Follow either of steps 6, 7 and 8.

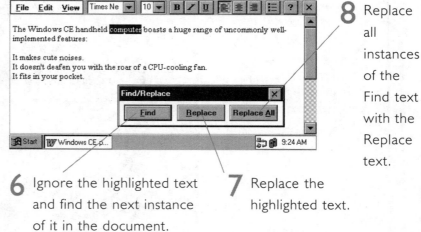

8 Replace all instances of the Find text with the Replace text.

6 Ignore the highlighted text and find the next instance of it in the document.

7 Replace the highlighted text.

File operations

Once you have created a document, you need to save it, so that you can return to it a later date, or so that the file can be transferred to a desktop PC. A saved file is accessed using the Open command, while a new file is created using the New command.

REMEMBER **Once you have saved a document for the first time, Pocket Word will perform any subsequent saves immediately, without asking you where to save the file or what name to give it. If you wish to save a file in a different folder or with a different name, choose Save As from the File menu instead.**

Saving a file

When you save a file for the first time, you are presented with the Save As dialog box. This lets you give a name to your document, and tell Pocket Word where you want to store it.

| Open the File menu and tap on Save.

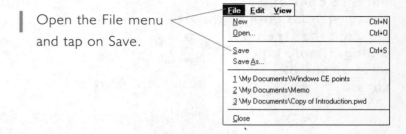

2 The Save As dialog box appears. Navigate to the folder in which you want to save your file, using the techniques discussed in Chapter Three.

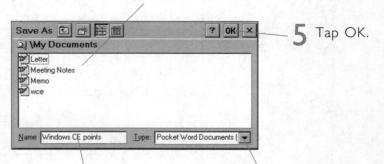

5 Tap OK.

HANDY TIP **You can save files using a keyboard shortcut instead of the File menu: press Control + S.**

3 Type in a name for your file.

4 If you prefer to save the document as a plain text file rather than a Pocket Word file, select the option from this drop-down list. (You may lose some of the document's formatting if you do this.)

Opening a saved file

Any Pocket Word files that have been saved by you or others can be opened easily, using the File menu. Pocket Word also understands plain text files.

1 Open the File menu and tap Open.

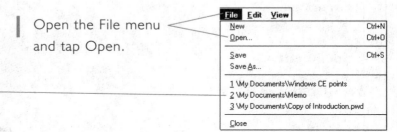

The files you have worked on most recently are shown here. To open any of these without going through the Open dialog, simply tap once on any of these.

2 The Open dialog box appears. Navigate to the folder that contains the file you want to open, using the techniques discussed in Chapter Three.

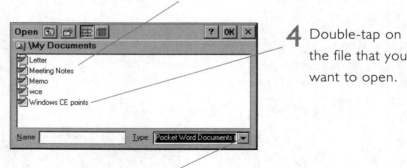

4 Double-tap on the file that you want to open.

3 If you want to open a plain text file instead of a Pocket Word document, select the option from this drop-down list.

Creating a new file

When you start the Pocket Word program, a new blank document is opened automatically, ready for you to type. If you wish to create a blank document at any other time, simply open the File menu and select New.

Using Outline view

So far, all the Pocket Word screens that we have seen have been in the default view. "Normal" view lets you easily enter text and change the font properties manually. However, there is an alternative view, called "Outline", which allows you to edit the structure of your document and its headings much more efficiently. To switch to Outline view, do the following:

1 Open the View menu.

2 Tap Outline.

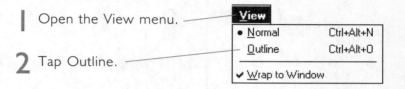

When the Outline view appears, you will notice that a small square box appears to the left of the first line of each paragraph. These are to help you see the structure of your document more clearly. You can change the properties of each paragraph using the Outline view's special icon bar, whose functions are shown below:

Promote heading

Revert to body text

Swap position of selected paragraph with paragraph below

Select which headings to view

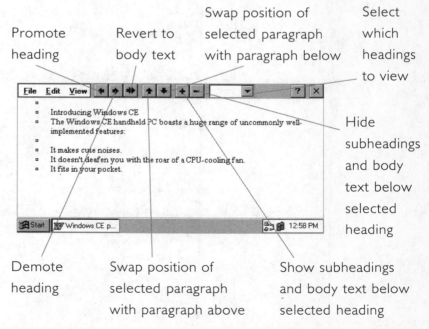

Hide subheadings and body text below selected heading

Demote heading

Swap position of selected paragraph with paragraph above

Show subheadings and body text below selected heading

1 Tap in a selected paragraph, then tap the "Promote heading" button.

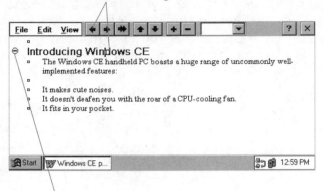

2 The font and font size of the paragraph are adjusted appropriately, and a minus sign now appears at its left in place of the square box, indicating that you may hide the details below this heading. Double-tap here...

3 ...and all but the heading are hidden. The plus sign here now shows that the heading contains text which may be revealed. Double-tap here to show its contents once more.

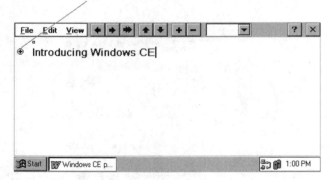

Sharing data with the desktop PC

When you transfer files between your desktop PC and the handheld, the files need to be converted, since Pocket Word files (*.pwd) and desktop Word files (*.doc) use a different format. Thankfully, HPC Explorer does this automatically. To copy a Pocket Word file to your desktop PC, open HPC Explorer and do the following:

REMEMBER

Chapter Eight explains in detail how to transfer files via a serial cable between the handheld and the desktop computer, using HPC Explorer.

1 Navigate to the file you wish to transfer, and select it.

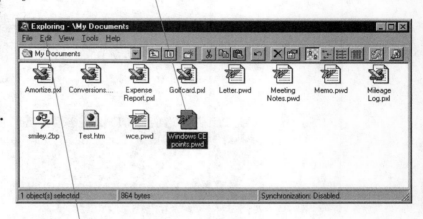

2 From the Edit menu, select Copy.

3 Open Windows Explorer and navigate to the directory where you want to place the Word file.

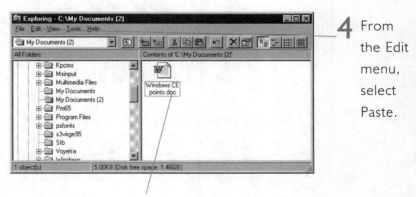

4 From the Edit menu, select Paste.

The file has automatically been converted to desktop Word's *.doc format.

If the file conversion doesn't work...

If you find that your Word or Pocket Word files are not converted when you transfer them between the handheld and the desktop, you may need to change the settings in HPC Explorer. In HPC Explorer, do the following:

1 Open the Tools menu and select File Conversion.

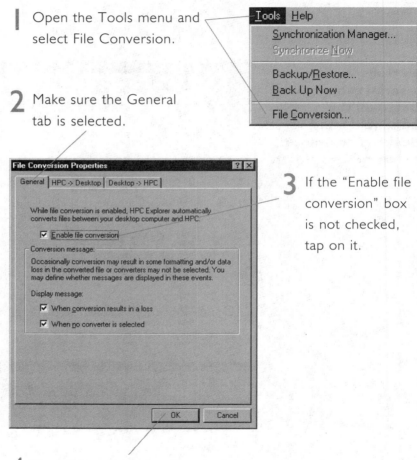

2 Make sure the General tab is selected.

3 If the "Enable file conversion" box is not checked, tap on it.

4 Tap OK to apply the change, then attempt the file conversion again.

Pocket Excel

Pocket Excel is a cut-down version of the desktop Excel spreadsheet program; it comes with every handheld PC running Windows CE. Despite the obvious memory restrictions that apply when working with such a small computer, Pocket Excel is packed with features, which should prove useful whether you're taking your business forecast to show your bank manager or keeping track of your golf scores.

Chapter Five

Covers

Overview

As with most modern computer spreadsheets, Pocket Excel is organised using a system of worksheets and workbooks. Worksheets are the grids in which you enter your figures and text, and the calculations based on them. The files in which the data is stored are known as workbooks, which contain any number of worksheets (memory allowing).

Pocket Excel lets you:

- Enter text or numbers in worksheet cells

- Apply functions and formulas to the numbers entered in selected cells, in order to perform automatic calculations

- Automatically fill in the contents of a range of cells based on the contents of the first cell, using Autofill

- Find and replace selected text or numbers

- Apply references to cells

All of these features will be covered in this chapter, and we will conclude by looking at how to exchange files between Pocket Excel and the desktop version.

Opening Pocket Excel

If the shortcut icon for Pocket Excel has been deleted from your main screen, tap the Start button, then select Programs and double-tap on the Microsoft Pocket Excel icon.

To open Pocket Excel, make sure the Windows CE main screen is visible and do the following:

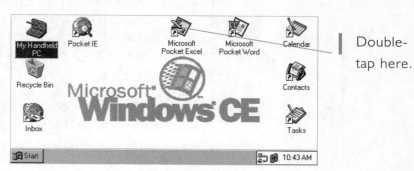

Double-tap here.

The Pocket Excel window opens, with a blank workbook ready for you to start entering data. The main components of the Window are outlined below:

Users of the desktop version of Excel will be used to having several workbooks open at the same time, each workbook having a separate window within the main Excel window. In Pocket Excel, you can have as many workbooks open as memory allows, but they appear as separate instances of the Pocket Excel program, each with its own button on the main Windows CE taskbar.

File, Edit, Format and Tools menus

File operation buttons

Cut, Copy and Paste buttons

Undo

Insert formula

Close window

Help

Scrollbars

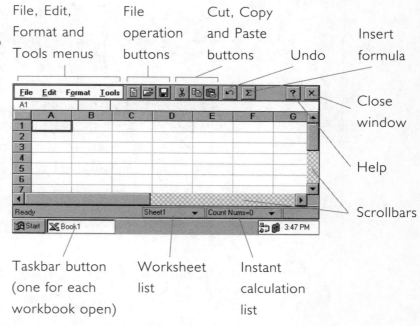

Taskbar button (one for each workbook open)

Worksheet list

Instant calculation list

Entering data

Before you can begin to use any of the fancy utilities provided by Pocket Excel, you need to enter some data. This is a simple process, requiring you to tap on the required cell and type in the desired data. Let us begin by entering some text and numbers into our first worksheet, which we will then use in later topics when we come to look at formulas and suchlike.

1 Using the stylus, tap on the cell where you want to enter some data. The cell is highlighted. Note that the cell reference is displayed in the box at the top-left of the window.

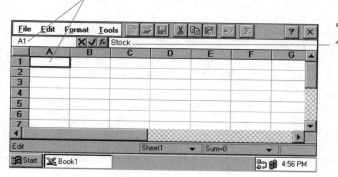

2 Enter some data using the keyboard. As you do so, the data appears in the Formula bar.

3 To accept what you have typed and enter it into the cell, tap on the tick mark, or simply move away from the current cell, as shown on the following page.

Moving around the worksheet

When you begin to enter data into the spreadsheet, you will need to know how to navigate around the worksheet, to move from one cell to another using the stylus and the keyboard. Using the stylus is easy: you simply tap on the cell you wish to edit. The keyboard commands, however, are a little more complicated:

Keyboard navigation

1 To move around the spreadsheet cell-by-cell, simply use the cursor arrow keys.

2 To move to the first cell in a row, press Control + Left arrow.

3 To move to the last cell in a row, press Control + Right arrow.

4 To move to the first cell in the spreadsheet, press Control + Up arrow.

5 To move to the last cell in the spreadsheet, press Control + Down arrow.

6 To move to any named cell in the worksheet, select Go To... from the Tools menu, then follow step 7.

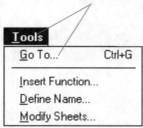

7 Enter the cell reference here, then tap OK.

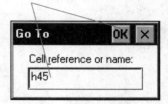

Introducing formulas and functions

So far you can enter text and numbers into your worksheet, but you haven't yet used Pocket Excel for what it is best at: automatically performing calculations based on the data you enter. This is based on the system of referencing cells by row and column. For example, let us say you had a value in cell A1 which you wished to add to a value in cell A2. You could insert a formula or function in cell A3 that would take the value of each cell and add them together; the calculated value would appear in A3, and the calculation would be revised if the contents of either cell A1 or A2 were amended. In fact, when you begin to enter a formula in a cell, Pocket Excel automatically guesses that you wish to add the contents of all the cells above it, as shown below:

1 Enter the values to be added in the appropriate cells.

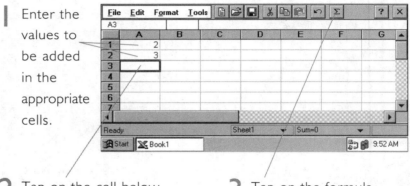

2 Tap on the cell below the last value.

3 Tap on the formula button.

4 Pocket Excel guesses that you want to add together the contents of the cell range A1 to A2. Tap on the tick button to confirm this.

REMEMBER

This is in fact a simple function, rather than a formula; see the topic "Entering functions".

...contd

The sum of cells A1 and A2 are shown in cell A3.

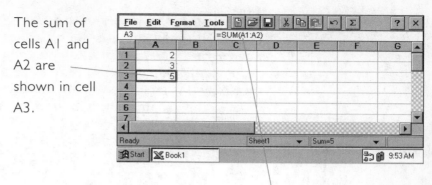

When a cell that contains a calculation is selected, the formula or function is shown here, in the Formula bar.

REMEMBER

To change any of the cell references for a formula or function, simply tap on the cell that contains the calculation, then tap in the Formula bar and edit its contents.

5 Try changing the value of one or more of the cells...

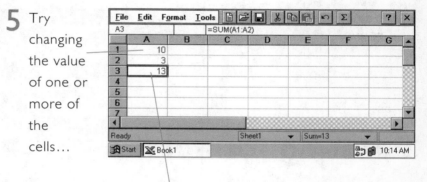

The value in cell A3 is updated automatically.

Entering cell ranges and groups of cells

You will notice that the contents of the Formula bar in the illustrations above reads:

=SUM(A1:A2)

This tells Pocket Excel to calculate the sum of the cells in the range A1 to A2. In this case, the range constitutes two cells only, but a range of any size could be used here instead. To add together any number of cells that are not in a range, use a comma instead of the colon, e.g.:

=SUM(A1,A3,B3)

Entering cell ranges using the stylus

If the cell range suggested automatically by Pocket Excel is not the one you want to use, you can enter it manually in the Formula bar. However, it is usually much easier to use the stylus. At step 4 in the previous topic, do the following before tapping on the tick button:

REMEMBER

As you can see here, the cell range is not restricted to a single column: it can span across any number of columns and rows.

1 Tap on the first cell in the range.

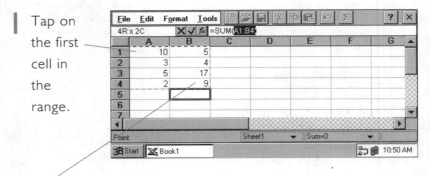

2 Without lifting the stylus from the screen, drag the selection area down to the last cell in the range.

Entering formulas

The calculations shown so far have used a function (SUM) to perform a very simple task – add the contents of a range of cells together. In fact, most functions are used to perform much more complex operations, as we shall see later. It is also possible to perform simple operations on numbers using *formulas*. While all functions have their own special name, which appears in the formula bar, formulas are comprised simply of cell references and/or numbers, which are acted on by *operators* used for addition, subtraction, division, etc. The most common operators recognised by Pocket Excel are:

Addition	+
Subtraction	-
Multiplication	*
Division	/

...contd

REMEMBER

You may be wondering how cells D2-D6 show the actual formulas and not their respective results. This is done by specifying manually that the values in that column are to be treated as text entries. For how to do this, see step 3 in the "Formatting cells" topic later.

Every formula must begin with '=', so that Pocket Excel knows that it is a formula and not simply a piece of text.

Some examples of formulas are shown in the worksheet below. Cells A2-B5 contain numerical values which are used (via cell references) in the formulas in column F. Cells D2-D6 show the actual formulas in cells F2-F6.

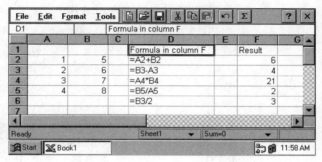

Entering functions

Functions are used to perform complex calculations on the contents of a cell or cells. They are grouped into eight categories:

Financial	Lookup
Date and Time	Text
Math and Trig	Logical
Statistical	Informational

It is not practical to detail each of the functions available in Pocket Excel here – there are over 100. For details on each of the functions, open Help by tapping on [?] in the top right-hand corner of the window, then select "Using functions" from the list of topics. An example of entering just one of Pocket Excel's functions is given overleaf.

Using the ROUND function

This is one of Pocket Excel's functions in the Math and Trigonometry category. ROUND allows you to take a number that contains a decimal fraction, either from a cell reference or by inputting it directly, and round off the fraction to a specified number of decimal places.

1 If you intend to round a number using a cell cross-reference, make sure the appropriate cell contains a value.

4 Tap on the Function button.

3 Tap on the Formula button.

2 Tap on the cell where you want the rounded value to appear.

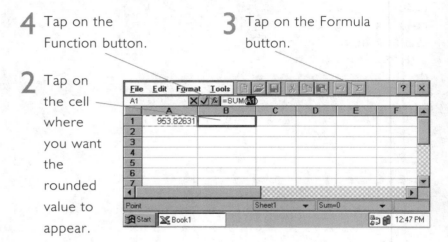

5 The Insert Function dialog box appears. Select the desired function category from this list.

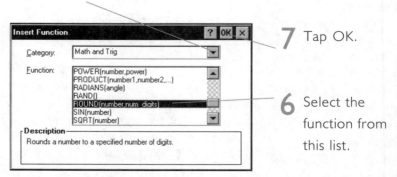

7 Tap OK.

6 Select the function from this list.

In the Formula bar, a ROUND function appears, with text fillers where you need to insert the two variables:

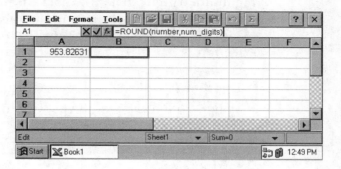

8 Tap in the Formula bar and replace the text 'number' with either a number or a cell reference.

Make sure you don't delete the comma that separates the two values.

In this topic we have looked at the application of just one of Pocket Excel's many functions. However, all other functions are inserted in the same basic fashion; the only differences lie in the type and number of variables required by each specific function.

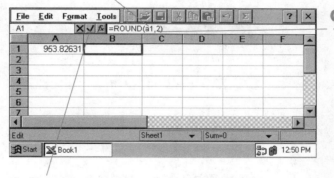

9 Replace the text 'num_digits' with the number of decimal places you want.

10 Tap here.

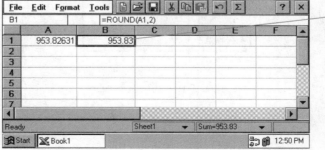

After step 10, the rounded value appears in the selected cell.

Filling cells automatically

When entering a lot of data into your worksheet, you may often have a predictable sequence of numbers which is very long and boring to type. In most cases, Pocket Excel can fill in the contents of such lists automatically, as long as you give it some information about the type of data you are entering.

1 Enter the first element of the sequence, then select that cell along with the cells which you wish to fill automatically.

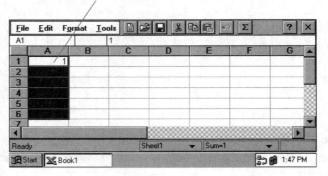

2 Open the Edit menu and select Fill.

3 The Fill dialog box appears. Select 'Series' as the Fill Type.

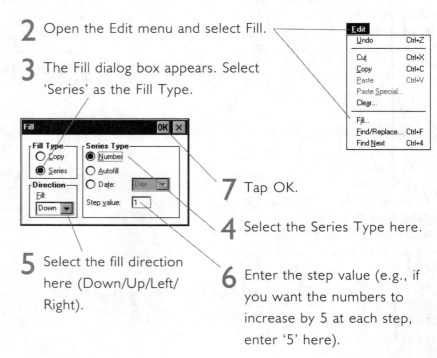

7 Tap OK.

4 Select the Series Type here.

5 Select the fill direction here (Down/Up/Left/Right).

6 Enter the step value (e.g., if you want the numbers to increase by 5 at each step, enter '5' here).

The
sequence
has been
filled in
automatically.

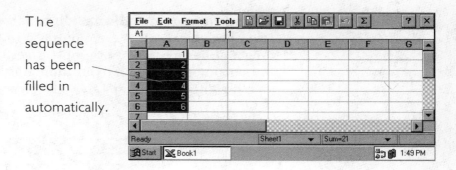

Working with rows and columns

By dealing with whole rows or columns, as opposed to single cells or small groups of cells, you can make many worksheet formatting tasks much easier.

Selecting rows or columns

In editing your worksheet, especially when adjusting its formatting, you will need to select whole rows or columns of data. To do this, you could tap your stylus at the first cell in the row or column, and drag it to the last cell – but that would take a very long time. There is a much easier way, as shown below. Do either of the following:

2 To select a whole row, tap on the number button at the left.

1 To select a whole column, tap on the letter button at the top.

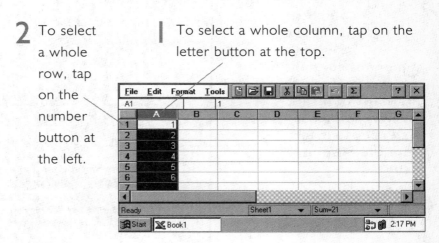

Changing row or column dimensions

Changing the width of a column or the height of a row is extremely easy in Pocket Excel. Do either of the following:

1 To change the column width, tap on the boundary between one column header button and the next, then drag the dividing line to the desired width.

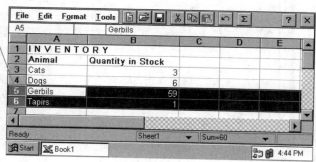

2 To change the height

of a row, tap on the boundary between one row header and the next, then drag the dividing line to the desired height.

Inserting rows or columns

If you find, once you have entered some data into your worksheet, that you need to insert some rows or columns, you don't need to erase everything and start again. To insert two rows, for instance, do the following:

To insert columns, select the required number of columns to the left of which you want to insert the new columns, then choose Insert from the Format menu

1 Select the two rows above which you want to insert the new rows.

2 From the Format menu, choose Insert.

Formatting cells

Once you have entered some data into your worksheet, you may want to change its format. For example, you can change the alignment of text within a cell, the font and font size with which it is displayed, and the border thickness of a selected range of cells. You can also alter the way in which selected data is treated by Pocket Excel – e.g. as text, currency, etc. To change any cell format properties, do the following:

1 Select the cell or range of cells whose format you want to change.

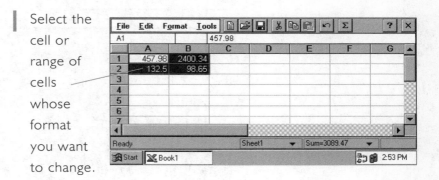

2 Open the Format menu and choose Cells

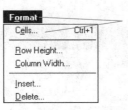

3 The Format Cells dialog appears. The Number tab allows you to select the way in which the numbers are to be treated. For example, 'Text', selected here, will treat any characters in the cell as plain text; any numbers will not be eligible for calculations, and formulae will display their actual structures, as opposed to their calculated values.

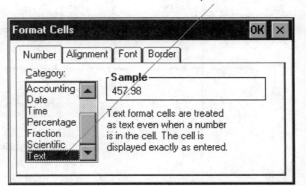

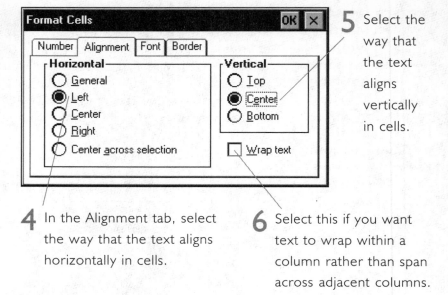

5 Select the way that the text aligns vertically in cells.

4 In the Alignment tab, select the way that the text aligns horizontally in cells.

6 Select this if you want text to wrap within a column rather than span across adjacent columns.

7 In the Font tab, select the font that you want to use in the selected cells.

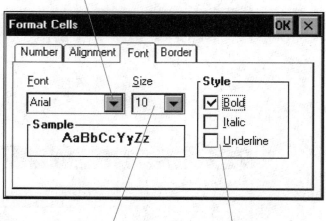

8 Select the point size of the text.

9 Choose whether the text should be bold, italic, underlined, or any combination of these.

...contd

Since the display of your handheld PC does not have a terribly high resolution, some of the bordering options you apply to cells may not be easily visible, depending on the screen's contrast settings.

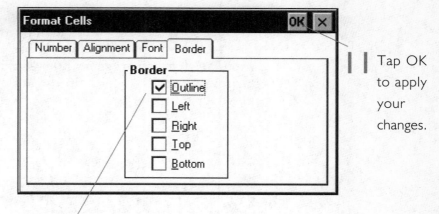

11 Tap OK to apply your changes.

10 The Border tab allows you to select the way in which the selected cells are bordered. Selecting Outline puts an outline around the selected cells; selecting left, for instance, puts a line along the left edge of each of the selected cells.

The cells below are set as text format (hence their left alignment, which is the default for text); the text is bold; and an outline has been applied around the whole group of cells.

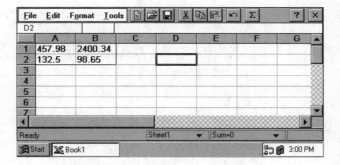

Using Find and Replace

Once you have entered some data into your worksheet, you may need to refer to it find out the value of some variable, or to track down an erroneous figure. If you have a particularly large worksheet, this could be a time-consuming process – without the aid of Pocket Excel's Find and Replace utility.

1 Open the Edit menu and select Find/Replace.

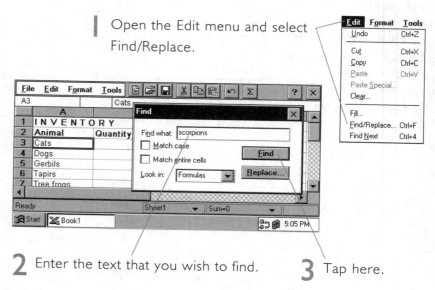

2 Enter the text that you wish to find.

3 Tap here.

4 The first instance of the text you entered is highlighted. To find the next, open the Edit menu again and choose Find Next.

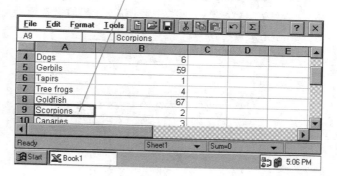

If you want to replace any found text, tap on the Replace button in the Find dialog (see step 3 on the previous page).

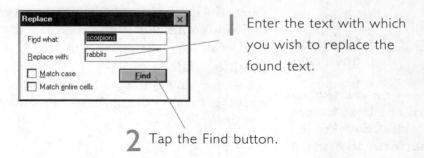

| Enter the text with which you wish to replace the found text.

2 Tap the Find button.

The Find/Replace bar appears, as shown below. This offers you three options:

| Tap here to ignore this instance of the found text and continue searching for other instances.

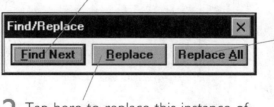

3 Tap here to replace all instances of the search text in the worksheet with the replacement text.

2 Tap here to replace this instance of the found text with the specified replacement text.

File operations

Once you have created a workbook, you need to save it, so that you can return to it a later date, or so that the file can be transferred to a desktop PC. A saved file is accessed using the Open command, while a new file is created using the New command.

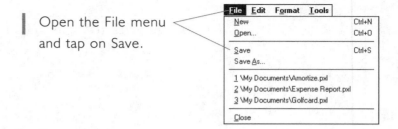
Once you have saved a workbook for the first time, Pocket Excel will perform any subsequent saves immediately, without asking you where to save the file or what name to give it. If you wish to save a file in a different folder of with a different name, choose Save As from the File menu instead.

Saving a file

When you save a file for the first time, you are presented with the Save As dialog box. This lets you give a name to your workbook, and tell Pocket Excel where you want to store it.

1 Open the File menu and tap on Save.

File	Edit	Format	Tools	
New				Ctrl+N
Open...				Ctrl+O
Save				Ctrl+S
Save As...				
1 \My Documents\Amortize.pxl				
2 \My Documents\Expense Report.pxl				
3 \My Documents\Golfcard.pxl				
Close				

2 The Save As dialog box appears. Navigate to the folder in which you want to save your file, using the techniques discussed in Chapter Three.

You can save files using a keyboard shortcut instead of the File menu: press Control + S.

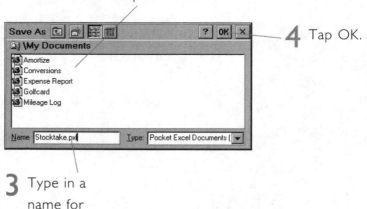

4 Tap OK.

3 Type in a name for your file.

Opening a saved a file

Any Pocket Excel files that have been saved by you or others can be opened easily, using the File menu.

HANDY TIP

The files you have worked on most recently are shown here. To open any of these without going through the Open dialog, simply tap once on its name.

| Open the File menu and tap on Open.

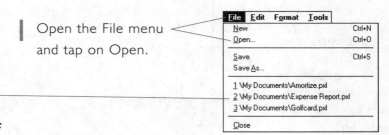

2 The Open dialog box appears. Navigate to the folder that contains the file you want to open, using the techniques discussed in Chapter Three.

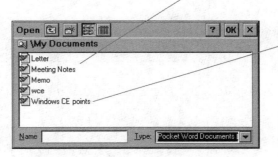

3 Double-tap on the file that you want to open.

Creating a new file

When you start the Pocket Excel program, a new blank workbook containing four worksheets is opened automatically, ready for you to start entering data. If you wish to create a blank workbook at any other time, simply open the File menu and select New.

Sharing data with the desktop PC

When you transfer files between your desktop PC and the handheld, the files need to be converted, since Pocket Excel files (*.pxl) and desktop Excel files (*.xls, *.xlb) use a different format. Thankfully, HPC Explorer does this automatically. To copy a Pocket Excel file to your desktop PC, open HPC Explorer and do the following:

REMEMBER

Chapter Eight explains in detail how to transfer files via a serial cable between the handheld and the desktop computer, using HPC Explorer.

2 From the Edit menu, select Copy.

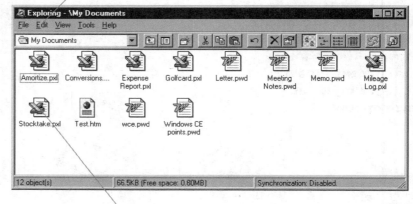

| Navigate to the file you wish to transfer, and select it.

3 Open Windows Explorer and navigate to the directory where you want to place the Excel file.

REMEMBER

If you find that you are having problems converting files between Pocket Excel and the desktop version of Excel, see "If the file conversion doesn't work" under the "Sharing data with the desktop PC" topic in Chapter Four.

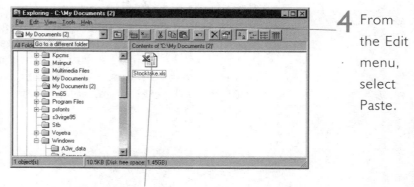

4 From the Edit menu, select Paste.

The file has automatically been converted to desktop Excel's *.xls format.

Chapter Six

Information Manager

Windows CE's Information Manager comprises three elements: Contacts, Calendar and Tasks. Between them, they allow you to organise your personal and business contacts, appointments and things to do. Although each is a separate application, they use similar interfaces so that you can quickly get to grips with using the whole suite of Information Manager programs.

Covers

Contacts – an overview

The Contacts program is designed to let you record information about all of your personal and business contacts. You can use it to store names, addresses telephone numbers and any other information you see fit, about any of your contacts.

Having this sort of information on your handheld PC means that you can throw away your dog-eared address book, your filofax, or your bundle of business cards; Contacts will allow you to handle this sort of information much more efficiently. Never again will you have to flick desperately through an old address book, trying to remember the surname of that important contact: Contacts can search through its whole database for instances of the most insubstantial snippets of information.

The information that you enter can be processed and sorted using Contacts' extremely versatile interface. In addition to the basic function of cataloguing your contacts by name, you can also sort the list by any of the other main categories: e.g., by company name or telephone number.

One particularly useful feature is that the names and email addresses you enter into Contacts can be imported very easily into Inbox, the Windows CE email program: see page 150 in Chapter Nine, "Internet Communications".

Opening Contacts

To open Contacts, make sure the Windows CE main screen is visible, and do the following:

 HANDY TIP **If the shortcut icon for Contacts has been deleted from your main screen, tap the Start button, then select Programs and double-tap on the Contacts icon.**

Double-tap here.

The Contacts window opens, displaying all the contacts that you have recorded so far. The main components of the window are indicated below:

File, Edit and Tools menus

New contact

Delete contact

Search contacts

Help

Close window

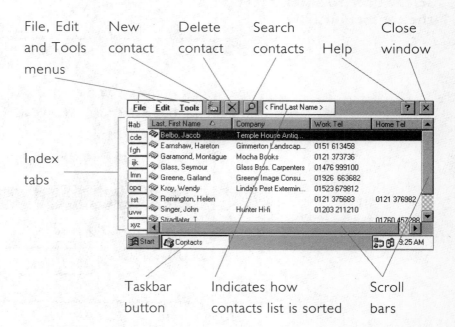

Index tabs

Taskbar button

Indicates how contacts list is sorted

Scroll bars

Adding and editing contacts

When you first start Contacts, the list of contacts in the main screen will be empty; you need to make some new entries before you can really begin using it. Do the following:

1 Tap on the New Contact button in the main window.

HANDY TIP

After you have entered a contact, you may want to edit its details. To do this, simply double-tap on it. This will then open the contact details screen used to enter the contact initially.

2 The following screen appears, with the Name section of the business tab highlighted. Type in a name.

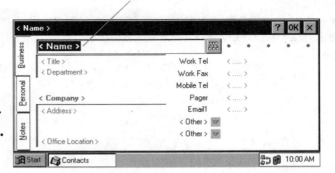

3 Depending on how you enter the name, you may be requested to confirm that Contact's analysis of its individual elements is correct. Make any amendments if necessary, then tap the OK button to confirm the new entry.

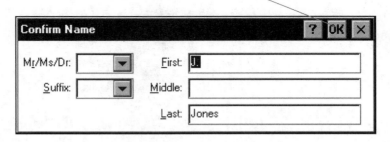

4 Enter any other information you have in the appropriate sections of the Business tab.

The contact details window shown on the previous page has three tabs: Business, Personal and Notes. You are not restricted to assigning each of your contacts to a single category; you can have business and personal information, as well as notes, for every contact entry, if you wish. To enter information in the Personal and Notes tabs, do the following:

5 Tap here.

6 Enter the contact's home address, telephone number, etc., in the appropriate boxes.

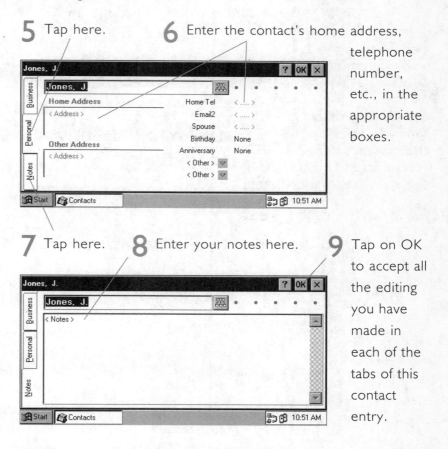

7 Tap here.

8 Enter your notes here.

9 Tap on OK to accept all the editing you have made in each of the tabs of this contact entry.

Editing and viewing contact entries

The screens used to edit and view contact entries are exactly the same as those shown on this page and the last – except, of course, they will already contain some information. To open the contact details window for any individual, simply double-tap on it in the contacts list.

Sorting the contacts list

By default, the contacts list is sorted in alphabetical order, by surname. However, you may find it more useful to sort it by any of the other three headings shown in the main list: Company, Work Telephone or Home Telephone. Sorting by telephone number, for example, could allow you to view all of your contacts by geographical area (using the area dialling code): this could be very useful for organising business trips or meetings with colleagues. To sort by any of these criteria, do the following:

Tap on any of these buttons.

The heading above the category used for the current sort order is marked with a ▲ symbol.

Deleting contacts

Any old or unwanted contacts can be deleted very easily. Do the following:

2 Tap here.

HANDY TIP

To select a group of consecutive entries in the contacts list, tap on the first in the group, then press the Shift key while tapping on the last. To select a number of non-consecutive entries, hold down the Control (CTRL) key while tapping on each one.

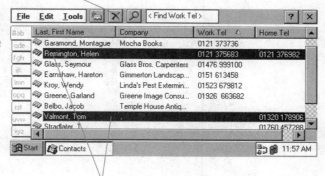

Select the file(s) you want to delete.

The following dialog box appears:

3 Tap here to delete the files, or...

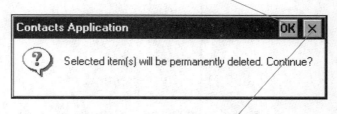

4 ...tap here to abort the delete operation and leave the selected contacts as they are.

Searching for contact data

If you can't find the required contact by sorting the main contact list, you can use the Find function to search for every instance of a piece of text in the whole contacts database. To do this, do the following:

| Tap here.

2 The Find dialog appears. Type the text you want to find in this box. (The search text can be in any of the contacts categories.)

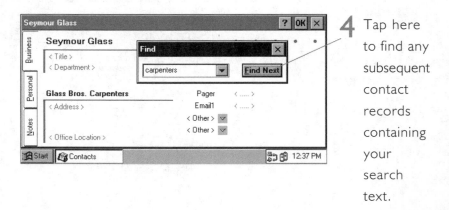

3 Tap here.

The first instance of text matching your search criteria is highlighted in the contact details view:

4 Tap here to find any subsequent contact records containing your search text.

The Calendar – an overview

The Information Manager's Calendar acts as a diary in which you can record details of all your personal and business appointments. You can use it to set an appointment for a lunch date half an hour in the future, or in five years' time, and then have it remind you with an alarm or a flashing light.

The Calendar offers you three views in which to manage your appointments: Day, Week and Agenda; it also provides a monthly calendar which you can use to navigate easily through your long-term itinerary.

You can schedule appointments or other events to last for any length of time: half an hour, two hours or all day. Using the weekly view, you can then see a graphic representation of how much of your week is booked up. One particularly helpful aspect of the Calendar is that it allows you to set recurring appointments for events that happen regularly: for example, weekly meetings or your daily lunch break.

All of these features mean that the Calendar is much more than an electronic notebook in which to record your appointments; it allows much more effective organisation, and can also act as an alarm clock and a personal assistant.

Opening the Calendar

To open the Calendar, do the following:

HANDY TIP **If the shortcut icon for the Calendar has been deleted from your main screen, tap the Start button, then select Programs and double-tap on the Calendar icon.**

Double-tap here.

The main Calendar window then opens, with the appointments for the current date on display. The main elements of the window are pointed out below:

File, Edit and View menus

Add new appointment

Delete appointment

View agenda

View daily schedule

View weekly schedule

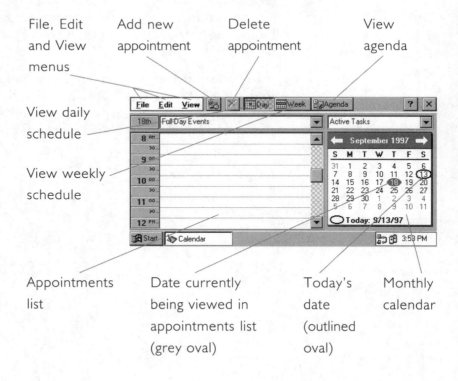

Appointments list

Date currently being viewed in appointments list (grey oval)

Today's date (outlined oval)

Monthly calendar

Adding and editing appointments

When you first start to use the Calendar, there will be no entries in the appointments list. To add an appointment, first navigate to the date on which it is to occur:

1 Tap on these arrows to advance or regress through the months of the calendar.

HANDY TIP

If it is not convenient to navigate to the month of the appointment using the monthly calendar view, you can jump directly to the appointment date by entering it with the keyboard. Select "Go to Date" from the View menu, enter the date in the dialog box, then tap OK.

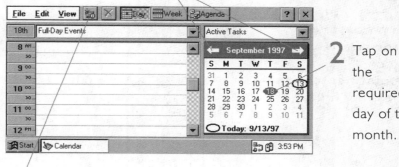

2 Tap on the required day of the month.

3 Tap on the Add Appointment button.

4 Enter a name and location for the appointment in these boxes.

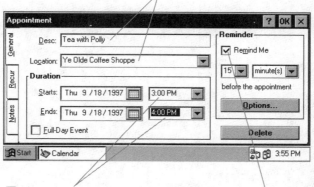

HANDY TIP

To edit an appointment after you have added it, double-tap on its entry in the Calendar; this summons the same window you used to create the appointment.

5 Enter the start and end times of the appointment.

6 If you want Calendar to remind you of your appointment, make sure this box is ticked and continue with the following steps. If you don't want any reminders, jump to step 15.

Some handheld PCs may not have the necessary hardware to warn you of appointments with a flashing light.

Setting reminders

The Notification Options dialog box allows you to select any or all of three ways to remind you when an appointment is about to occur: it can set off an audible alarm, alert you with an on-screen message, or flash the special warning light on your handheld's case. To set these, do the following:

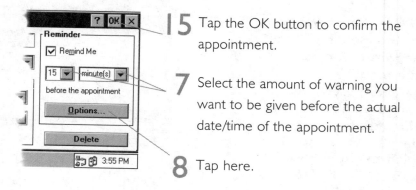

15 Tap the OK button to confirm the appointment.

7 Select the amount of warning you want to be given before the actual date/time of the appointment.

8 Tap here.

10 If you followed step 9, select the alarm sound to use.

14 Tap OK.

9 Tick this box if you want to be warned with a sound.

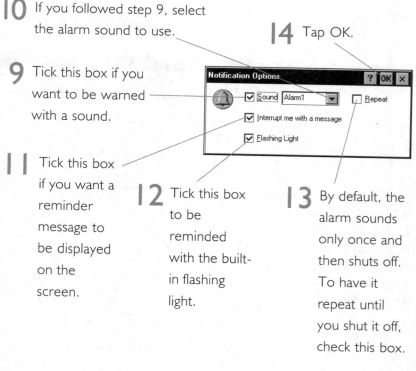

11 Tick this box if you want a reminder message to be displayed on the screen.

12 Tick this box to be reminded with the built-in flashing light.

13 By default, the alarm sounds only once and then shuts off. To have it repeat until you shut it off, check this box.

Setting recurring appointments

Many of your appointments are likely to recur daily, weekly or monthly. Calendar saves you the task of entering such appointments many times for different dates by allowing you to specify how often an appointment should recur; after you have set the details for the first appointment, Calendar fills in the rest automatically, using the same properties except for the date. If you wish to set a recurring appointment, do the following before tapping OK in step 15 on the previous page:

2 By default, the Recur value is set to 'Once'. To make the appointment recur, select one of the other options.

1 Tap the Recur tab.

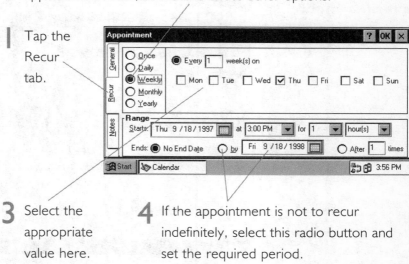

3 Select the appropriate value here. The available options depend on which type of recurrence you selected in step 2.

4 If the appointment is not to recur indefinitely, select this radio button and set the required period.

Setting all-day appointments

If an appointment is due to last all day, you don't need to set the whole time range manually. Instead, you can simply check a box which sets aside the day automatically.

1 Use the techniques shown in the 'Adding and editing appointments' topic to navigate to the day of the appointment.

2 Tap on this arrow button and select New Full Day Event from the drop-down list.

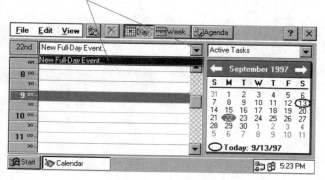

3 The Appointment dialog box appears, with the Full-Day Event box ticked.

4 Enter a description for the event, and a location if applicable.

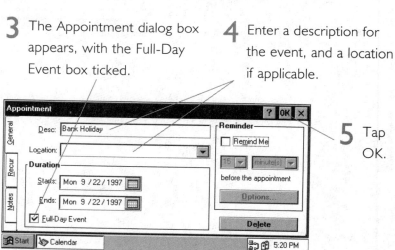

5 Tap OK.

The text in
this box has
now changed
to reflect the
description
of the full-
day event
you have just
entered .

Switching between Calendar views

So far, we have only used one of Calendar's views: daily
view. This is designed to allow you to view the structure of
your appointments for a single day, in the greatest detail.
However, there are two other views: 'weekly' and 'agenda'.

Weekly view

If you need to compare your appointments over the scale of
a whole week, you should switch to weekly view. Do the
following:

Tap on this button, or choose 'Week' from the View menu.

The monthly calendar disappears to make way for the rest of the days of the week. As in the daily view, the space allocated for each of the appointments is determined by the amount of time they take up. If you can't make out what an appointment is from the text that is displayed, double-tap on it to reveal the full appointment details screen.

Tap on the heading button for any particular day to switch back to the daily view for that day.

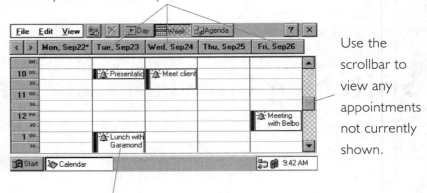

Use the scrollbar to view any appointments not currently shown.

Double-tap on any of the appointments to switch to the appointment details screen.

In the screen shown above, only the days Monday to Friday are shown. However, if you prefer, you can view the whole seven-day week:

In the View menu, tap here to remove the tick from the '5-Day Week View' entry.

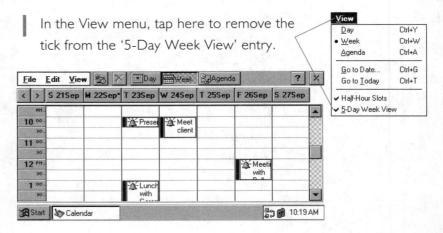

...contd

Agenda view

If you simply need a plain list of your appointments, without the graphical time-scale layout of the daily and weekly views, you can use the agenda view.

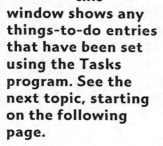

The Active Tasks section of this window shows any things-to-do entries that have been set using the Tasks program. See the next topic, starting on the following page.

1 Tap on this button, or choose 'Agenda' from the View menu.

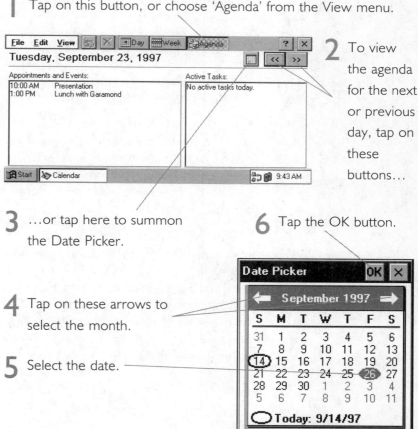

2 To view the agenda for the next or previous day, tap on these buttons...

3 ...or tap here to summon the Date Picker.

4 Tap on these arrows to select the month.

5 Select the date.

6 Tap the OK button.

The agenda view does not allow you to edit your appointments, directly or indirectly; double-tapping on an appointment's entry does not summon the appointment details screen. To edit any entries, you need to switch back to daily or weekly view first.

Tasks – an overview

While the Calendar program allows you to keep track of
appointments or other events that have a specific start and
end time, Tasks lets you create a list of things to do which
can be checked off as you complete them. The interface
used is very similar to that of the Calendar, but does not
provide a facility for entering specific times of the tasks
you wish to set.

Just as with the Calendar, you can set reminders to alert
you when a task should be begun, or when it is due to be
finished. Again, a reminder can take the form of an audible
alarm, an on-screen message or a flashing light.

For each task, you can set the dates between which the task
is to be performed, and then sort the task list to see which
of your tasks should be dealt with next. Once a task has
been completed, you can tick it off, just as you would on a
piece of paper; you will then not be bothered by any more
reminder alarms.

If you are a particularly busy person, you may have several
tasks due for completion at around the same time. For
example, you might have a project at work to complete,
while at home you may also have set yourself the tasks of
wallpapering the spare bedroom and giving the dog a bath.
In order to resolve this conflict, the Tasks program allows
you to assign different priority levels to each task so that
you know which should really be carried out first.

Opening Tasks

To open Tasks, make sure the Windows CE main screen is visible and do the following:

HANDY TIP If the shortcut icon for Tasks has been deleted from your main screen, tap the Start button, then select Programs and double-tap on the Tasks icon.

Double-tap here.

The Tasks window opens, displaying all the tasks that you have set so far. The main elements of the window are pointed out below.

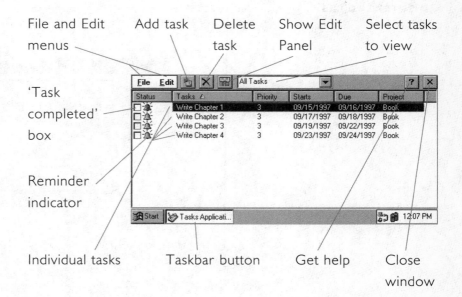

File and Edit menus

Add task

Delete task

Show Edit Panel

Select tasks to view

'Task completed' box

Reminder indicator

Individual tasks

Taskbar button

Get help

Close window

Adding and editing tasks

When you start the Tasks program for the first time, the task list will be empty. To create a task, do the following:

1 Tap here.

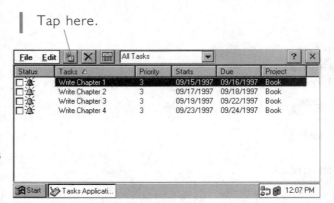

After you have entered a task, you may want to edit its details. To do this, simply double-tap on it. This will then open the task details screen used to enter the task initially.

2 Enter a name for the task.

3 If this task is part of a project, enter the project's name here, or select one from the list of previously-used project names.

4 Choose a priority rating for the task. (The default is 3.)

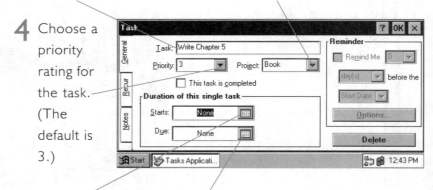

5 Select the date on which you should begin the task, and the date on which you should complete it.

Re step 5: Locate the correct date in the Date Picker, then tap the OK button.

6 If you want to be reminded when a task should be started, make sure this box is ticked (tap it if it isn't), then refer to the steps under the sub-heading "Setting reminders" on page 88.

Setting recurring tasks

If you need to repeat the same task on a regular basis, you don't have to add many identical entries to the task list for different dates. Instead, you can use the Recur tab of the task details screen to insert the tasks automatically.

2 By default, the Recur value is set to 'Once'. To make the appointment recur, select one of the other options.

1 Tap the Recur tab.

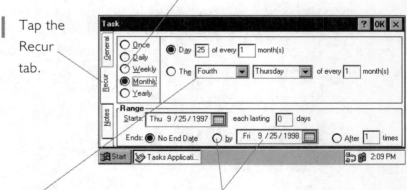

3 Select the appropriate value here. The available options depend on which type of recurrence you selected in step 2.

4 If the task is not to recur indefinitely, select this radio button and set the required period.

Sorting the task list

By default, the task list is sorted by task name (using the contents of the 'Task' column), in alphabetical order. However, there are five other columns – Status, Priority, Starts, Due and Project – by which you can sort the task list instead, if you prefer. For example, if you sort the list by the contents of the 'Due' column, you will see your tasks in the order in which they need to be performed. To sort the task list, do the following:

Tap on any of these buttons.

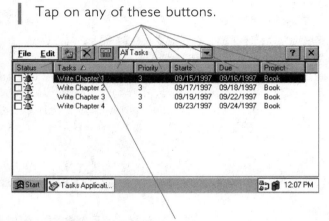

The heading above the category used for the current sort order is marked with a ▲ symbol.

Using the Edit panel

The task list in the main Tasks window gives you basic information on each task, in a truncated form; detailed editing is done via the task details screen that we saw in the "Adding and editing tasks" topic. However, you can also edit the basic details of a task using the Edit panel, which, when activated, is shown on the same screen as the main task list. To use the Edit panel, do the following:

1 Tap here.

2 To edit any of these details, simply tap on the text and enter your amendments.

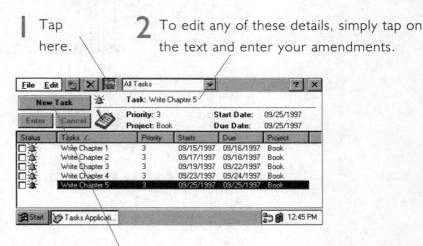

3 To create a new task, tap here. This will allow you to enter the basic details of the new task directly in the Edit panel. If you then want to edit properties which the Edit panel does not show (e.g. reminder alarm settings), you should double-tap on its entry in the task list to open the task details screen (as in the "Adding and editing tasks" topic).

Marking tasks as completed

When you have finished a task, you should mark it as completed. This will disable any reminder alarms that you might have set, and will help you to manage your schedule for those tasks that are not yet completed. Do the following:

Tap on the box to the left of the task that is completed, so that a tick appears.

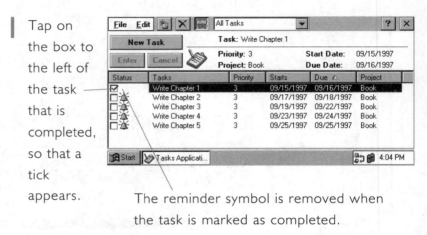

The reminder symbol is removed when the task is marked as completed.

The entry for a task is not deleted as soon as you mark it as completed; you must delete it manually, once you are sure that you will not want to refer to it in the future. To delete a single completed task, follow step 1 below; to delete all the tasks that have been marked as completed, follow step 2.

1 Select the task that you want to delete, then tap on the Delete button (☒) in the toolbar.

2 Open the Edit menu, then tap on "Delete Completed Tasks".

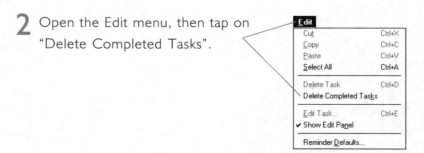

Customising Windows CE

Just as with the desktop version of Windows, there is plenty that you can do to adapt Windows CE to your style of working, and to give it that personal touch. For example, you can change the appearance of Windows CE, the way it sounds, and the way it manages its memory resources.

Covers

Chapter Seven

The Control Panel

So far, we have looked almost exclusively at how to operate the main utilities that are a part of the Windows CE package: Pocket Word, Pocket Excel and the three-part Information Manager. All of these use Windows CE as a medium in which to operate. However, we have not yet considered how to alter the settings of Windows CE itself. Many settings made to the operating system affect all of the applications that run on it.

Most of these sorts of changes are made using the Control Panel, which is a collection of utilities that each deal with a specific part of the workings of your handheld PC. To open the Control Panel, do the following:

| Open the Start menu and tap on Settings.

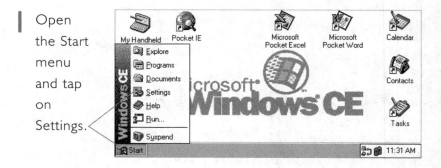

The Control Panel appears. This is really just a system folder which contains a number of special icons. Some of the functions available here will already be familiar to you, since you were required to enter some setup information the first time you turned on your handheld PC; other functions are dealt with in other chapters.

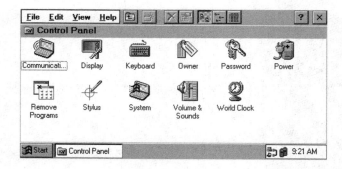

REMEMBER

The Control Panel folder is viewed using the Windows CE Explorer; see Chapter Three, "Managing Files and Folders", for more details on how to use this file-management application.

2 For a brief explanation of the function of each of the Control Panel utilities, tap on the File Details button.

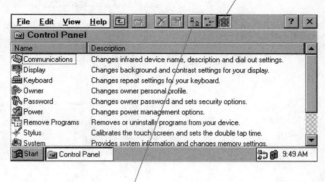

3 To return to the normal Control Panel view, tap on the Large Icons button.

Display

This utility contains two tabs, labelled 'Background' and 'Contrast'. The first lets you customise the appearance of Windows CE's main screen by changing the image which is used to decorate it.

Background

1 Double-tap on the Display icon in the Control Panel.

Preview of currently selected background image

2 In the Background tab, tap on this button.

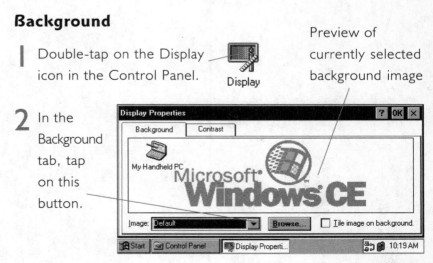

6 Tap OK to apply your changes to the background.

3 Select a new image from the list.

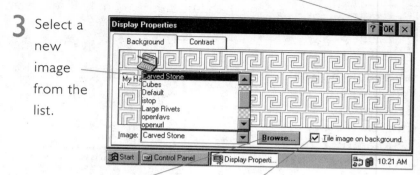

4 The images in the list are located in the My Handheld PC\Windows folder. If you have an image in another location which you wish to use, tap here to locate it.

5 Tick this box (by tapping on it) if you want the image to be tiled across the whole background. (A non-tiled image will be displayed once, in the centre of the background.)

Here, the 'Carved Stone' image has been tiled across the background:

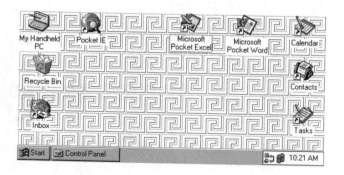

Contrast

The Contrast tab provides instructions on how to adjust the difference between the shades of grey on your handheld PC. This depends on the specifications of the hardware you are using. Many handheld units will have a contrast wheel on the side of the casing; you adjust the contrast simply by turning this, and do not change the contrast using the Windows CE operating system. Other units may allow you to alter the contrast by tapping on-screen adjuster buttons.

To display the Contrast tab, follow the steps below:

1 Double-tap on the Display icon in the Control Panel.

Display

2 Tap on this tab.

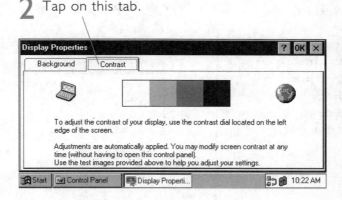

The images on this screen allow you to adjust the contrast to give the best distinction between the shades of grey that the handheld can display.

Keyboard

When you press and hold down a key on your handheld's keyboard, it initially enters one character in the application you are using; after a short pause, it then repeats that character rapidly, for as long as you hold down the key. This feature is particularly useful when, say, you are using a word-processor and wish to enter many spaces on a line without tapping the space key repeatedly.

The Keyboard utility in the Control Panel allows you to change the length of the pause before the characters are repeated, and the rate at which they are repeated. Follow these steps:

I   Double-tap on the Keyboard
     icon in the Control Panel.

Keyboard

Re steps 3 and 4: as an alternative to tapping on the arrow buttons, just tap on the slide adjuster and drag it to the desired point on the scale.

3   Tap on these arrows to adjust the length of the pause before characters are repeated.

2   Tick or untick this box depending on whether or not you want characters to repeat when you hold down a key.

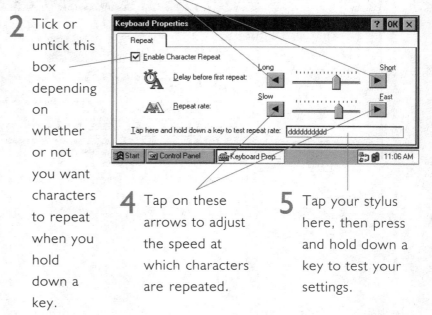

4   Tap on these arrows to adjust the speed at which characters are repeated.

5   Tap your stylus here, then press and hold down a key to test your settings.

Password

By default, when you turn on your handheld PC, the main Windows CE screen is shown immediately, allowing you access to all the applications on it. However, if you wish to prevent others from using your handheld without your permission, you can set a password which must be entered every time Windows CE is started.

1 Double-tap on the Password icon in the Control Panel.

Password

2 Enter a password in this box.

3 Enter the password again here, to confirm that you entered it correctly in step 2.

5 Tap OK.

HANDY TIP

To turn off password protection, untick the box in step 4.

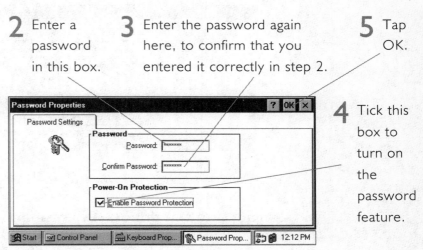

4 Tick this box to turn on the password feature.

BEWARE

Remember your password! If you forget it, you will not be able to use Windows CE without performing a complete hardware reset of your handheld PC.

Whenever you turn on your handheld PC now, you must enter your password before being allowed to progress any further.

Enter your password here, then hit Return or tap OK.

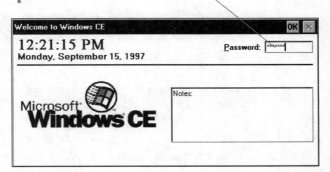

Stylus

When you first set up Windows CE, you were required to
calibrate the stylus-detection mechanism. If you experience
problems with the way that Windows CE detects your stylus
actions, you might need to recalibrate it. You can also
change the settings used for the double-tap stylus action.

Double-tap on the Stylus icon in the Control
Panel to open the Stylus Properties window.

Stylus

Recalibrating the stylus

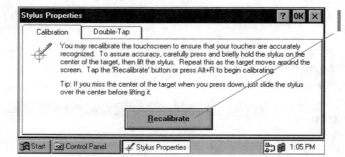

Make sure
the
Calibration
tab is
active, then
tap on this
button.

2 Follow the steps given on page 9 in Chapter 1.

Setting the double-tap properties

Double-tap on this square at the speed at which you want
your double-taps to be measured in the future.

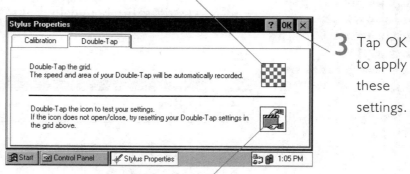

3 Tap OK
to apply
these
settings.

2 Test the settings by double-tapping this icon. If your
double-tap is recognised, it should change to this:

Changing memory allocation

Unlike your desktop PC, which uses one component (the hard drive) for the long-term storage of data and another (the bank of RAM chips) for actively processing it, your handheld PC performs both functions using a single basic memory component. Nevertheless, your handheld divides its memory into two categories: storage memory (analogous to your desktop PC's hard drive) and program memory (analogous to RAM). You can define how the memory is divided between the two types using the following method:

1 Double-tap on the System icon in the Control Panel.

System

REMEMBER

Don't worry that you might accidentally reallocate some memory that is already in use, and hence interfere with an active program or destroy some stored data: if you drag the slider within the used (grey) areas, it just bounces back out again, into the free (black) area.

2 Select the Memory tab.

4 Tap the OK button.

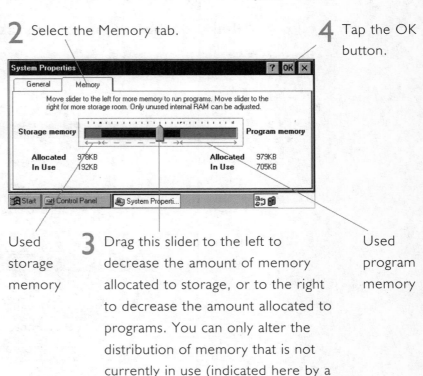

Used storage memory

3 Drag this slider to the left to decrease the amount of memory allocated to storage, or to the right to decrease the amount allocated to programs. You can only alter the distribution of memory that is not currently in use (indicated here by a dotted line).

Used program memory

Volume & Sounds

When certain events occur in Windows CE, such as when the operating system starts after you reset the handheld, or when you perform an illegal action in an application, an action-specific sound is usually played. You can change which sounds are played for each system event, and the volume at which they are played. These properties are amended using the Volume & Sounds Properties window, which is opened as follows:

Double-tap on the Volume & Sounds icon in the Control Panel.

Volume & Sounds

Adjusting the volume of sounds

1 Make sure the Volume tab is active.

2 To adjust the overall volume level, drag the slider up or down, or tap on the arrows.

5 Tap the OK button.

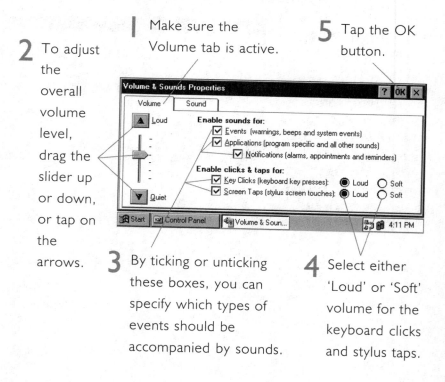

3 By ticking or unticking these boxes, you can specify which types of events should be accompanied by sounds.

4 Select either 'Loud' or 'Soft' volume for the keyboard clicks and stylus taps.

...contd

Changing the sounds used

REMEMBER

Every event that currently has a sound assigned to it is marked with this icon: 🔊

2 Tap on the event for which you wish to change the sound.

| Tap on the Sounds tab.

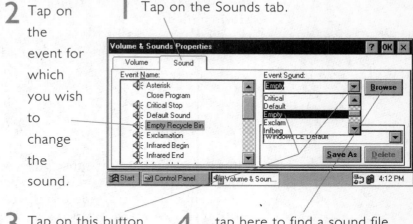

3 Tap on this button and select a sound from the list, or...

4 ...tap here to find a sound file (with the *.wav file extension) stored in any folder.

HANDY TIP

The default sound scheme does not assign sounds to all the events recognised by Windows CE. To have every event accompanied by a sound, choose the scheme 'All Sounds' from the list of schemes.

Windows CE, like the desktop version of Windows, lets you save a record of the sounds assigned to a set of events, using *sound schemes*. You can save any number of different sound schemes, and switch between them as you wish; this allows you to change the sounds for a whole range of events in a single action. Do the following to save a sound scheme:

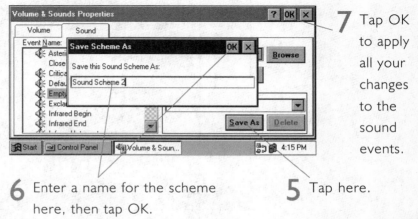

7 Tap OK to apply all your changes to the sound events.

6 Enter a name for the scheme here, then tap OK.

5 Tap here.

Installing extra fonts

You will probably have noticed that the number of fonts installed on your handheld PC is very small compared to the number on your desktop PC; by default, the following are installed:

- Arial
- Comic Sans MS
- Courier New
- MS Sans Serif

- Symbol
- Terminal
- Times New Roman
- Wingdings

These are adequate for most purposes, especially considering that most material created on the handheld will eventually be uploaded to the desktop PC for further editing. However, you can install any of the desktop's fonts onto the handheld, using the HPC Explorer. Do the following:

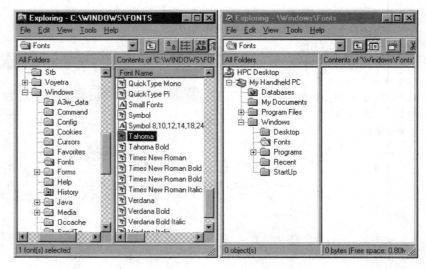

REMEMBER

Chapter Eight explains how to establish a connection between the handheld and the desktop PC, using the serial cable and HPC Explorer.

1 Establish a connection between the handheld and the desktop PC; use HPC Explorer to open the Windows\Fonts folder on the handheld.

2 Open the desktop Windows Explorer and navigate to the C:\Windows\Fonts folder.

3 Select the font(s) that you want to install, then drag them with the mouse over into the Fonts folder on the handheld.

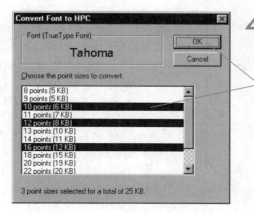

4 HPC Explorer prompts you to select which point sizes of the font you require; some suggested sizes are selected automatically for you. Tap on any entry to select or deselect it, then tap OK.

HPC Explorer begins to convert the fonts automatically:

The desktop PC's font files are converted automatically to the format used by the handheld: *.FNT.

One file is created in the Windows/Fonts folder for each of the font's point sizes. In this case, the three files created take up 25k of the handheld's storage.

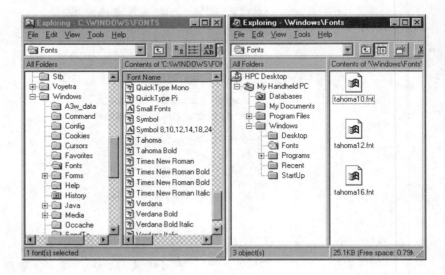

When you open any of your applications that use fonts now, you will see the new font in the font list. Note in this case that only the three font sizes that were chosen are available in the font size list.

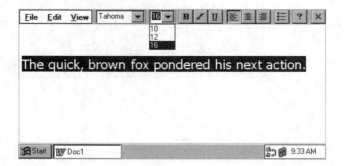

Handheld/Desktop PC Communications

A handheld PC running Windows CE can be a useful tool in its own right: you can use it to organise your timetable, perform spreadsheet calculations, write notes or letters, act as a reminder system, and many other things. However, once you begin to take advantage of the fact that you can exchange data on the handheld with your desktop PC, the possibilities are much more exciting: many of the computer tasks that you once had to perform at your desk can now be done anywhere. To achieve this communication you need to use a program on your PC called HPC Explorer, whose functions are explained in this chapter.

Covers

HPC Explorer – an overview

When you bought your handheld PC it should have come with an RS232C serial cable. The smaller plug connects to a port on the side of your handheld; the larger one plugs into the back of your desktop PC – see the manufacturer's instructions for precise details on how to do this.

Once you have plugged in the cable at both ends and you have turned on both computers, nothing happens; you need to install and run the HPC Explorer program on your desktop PC.

HPC Explorer closely resembles the Explorer utility that is present on both your desktop PC and your handheld: it displays a window showing the folder structure of a computer's storage space, and the details of the files in any selected folder. The special thing about HPC Explorer is that, while the program runs on your desktop PC, the files and folders it looks at are located on your handheld.

HPC Explorer allows you to copy files from the handheld to the desktop PC, and vice versa, using the normal click-and-drag method you will be familiar with in all versions of Windows. However, when you copy a file from one computer to another, in many cases it isn't simply copied; its format is also translated, so that it can be read by the appropriate application on the other computer. For example, the version of Word that you use on your desktop computer incorporates many features (such as coloured or rotated text) that are not handled by Pocket Word; so when HPC Explorer converts a file into Pocket Word format, any such enhancements need to be filtered out so that the handheld PC can handle the file. All this is done automatically, if HPC Explorer has been set up to perform translations for the file type being copied.

Before you can begin to use HPC Explorer, you need to install it – this is the subject of the next topic.

Installing HPC Explorer

To install HPC Explorer, you need the Windows CE CD-ROM. Insert it into the desktop PC's CD-ROM drive. If AutoPlay is enabled on your PC, you should see the window below; if not, follow step 1:

| Select "Run" from the Start menu. Click on the Browse button, and locate the CD-ROM drive, then run the file in its root directory called "Setup.exe" (the ".exe" extension may not be shown).

REMEMBER

The most up-to-date version of HPC Explorer can always be downloaded from the Internet, at:

http://
www.microsoft.com/
windowsce/hpc/
software/
hpcexplorer.htm

See the topic "Downloading from the Internet" in Chapter Two for how to download software.

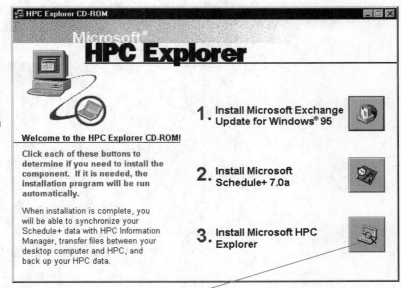

2 Click here.

3 The Setup wizard then installs HPC Explorer automatically. Follow any on-screen commands it gives you. When it has finished, you need to tell the wizard about the communications port you intend to use to connect to the handheld PC…

4 Click here; in the drop-down list, select the serial port on your desktop PC into which you will plug the RS232C cable.

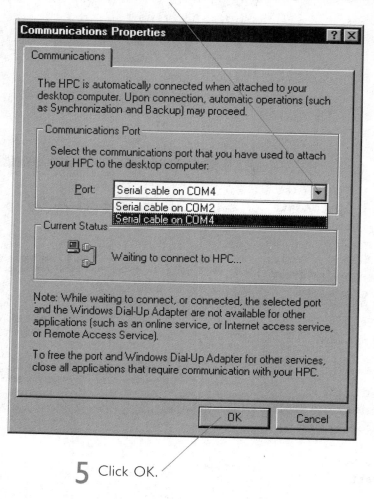

5 Click OK.

HPC Explorer will now attempt to connect to the handheld PC. The procedure you should follow for using HPC Explorer is the same as when you run it on any subsequent occasion, as explained on the following page.

Running HPC Explorer

To start HPC Explorer, do the following:

| Click on the Start button and choose Programs>HPC Explorer>HPC Explorer.

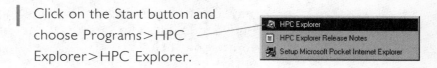

HPC Explorer automatically attempts to establish a connection with the handheld PC, displaying the window below. If you have not already plugged the serial cable into both the handheld PC and the desktop PC, do so now.

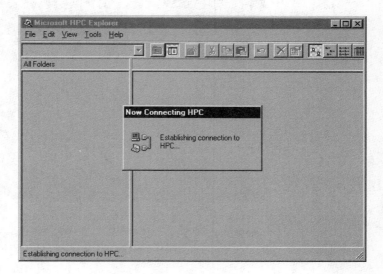

Be patient. The process of establishing the connection, testing it, and then reading the contents of the folders on the handheld PC takes a while – normally around 30 seconds.

Once the connection has been established properly, the following window appears (though the files and/or folders may differ, depending on how you have arranged them on your handheld). The various elements of the screen are pointed out below:

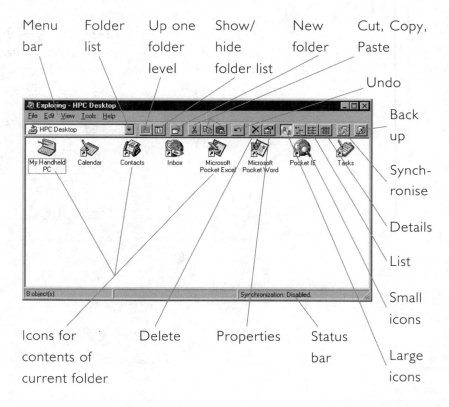

Menu bar | Folder list | Up one folder level | Show/ hide folder list | New folder | Cut, Copy, Paste | Undo | Back up | Synch-ronise | Details | List | Small icons | Large icons

Icons for contents of current folder | Delete | Properties | Status bar

You should recognise the icons displayed here: the folder shown when HPC Explorer is started up is a display of the contents of your handheld's main screen (except for the Recycle Bin).

HPC Explorer allows you to explore the contents of all of the folders on your handheld PC. You can also move them, delete them and view their properties. However, you can't use HPC Explorer to do everything that Windows CE Explorer can. Most significantly, you can't open files that are located on the handheld; they must be copied to the desktop first. Double-clicking on an icon does not open that program or document, but displays its properties:

If you double-clicked on a shortcut, you can select this tab to display the target location of the shortcut.

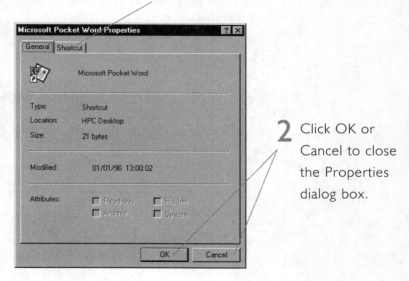

2 Click OK or Cancel to close the Properties dialog box.

Changing views

By default, HPC Explorer displays the contents of a single folder in a single pane; double-tapping on a folder's icon then causes the window to display the contents of that folder – like the interface of the My Computer utility in the desktop version of Windows. However, HPC Explorer also has a two-pane view similar to that of Windows Explorer, the left-hand pane displaying the tree-structure of the folders, and the right-hand pane displaying the contents of any selected folder. If the HPC Explorer window is slow to update as you move through the folders, using the folder view allows you to speed up navigation by displaying all of the folders at the same time. To display the folder-view, do the following:

1 Click here, or open the View menu and select Folders.

2 Click on the plus or minus signs to reveal or hide sub-folders.

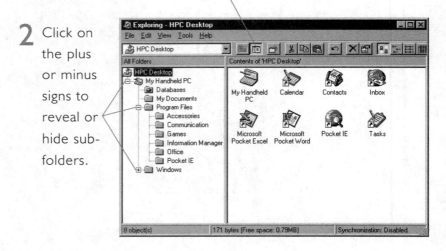

If a folder contains any sub-folders, a box containing a plus or minus sign will be displayed to the left of that folder's icon in the left-hand pane. A plus sign indicates that more sub-folders can be displayed; a minus sign indicates that the folder's sub-folders can be hidden. To reveal or hide the sub-folders, just click on the plus or minus sign, as in step 2 above.

Copying and moving files internally

HPC Explorer can do more than just swap data between the handheld and the desktop PC; you can use it as a kind of remote Windows CE Explorer to arrange the structure of the files on your handheld PC. The methods you use to do this are just the same as with Windows Explorer. For example, to move a file from one folder to another, you can use the following method (amongst others):

1 Right-click on the file you want to move.

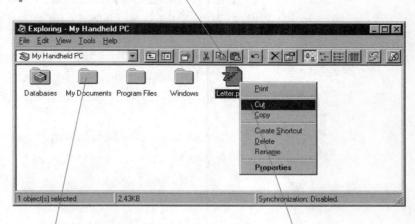

3 Move to the folder into which you want to move the file.

2 In the pop-up menu, select Cut.

4 Right-click anywhere within the folder window and select Paste from the pop-up menu.

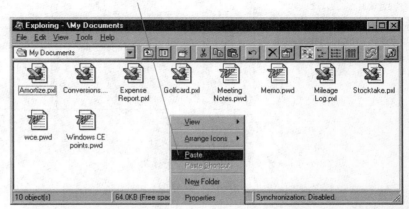

Exchanging files with the handheld

Copying or moving files between the handheld and the desktop PC is just as simple, from the user's point of view, as moving them internally within the handheld's storage memory; all the translation of file-types is done in the background by the HPC Explorer software.

Examples of converting Pocket Word and Pocket Excel files to their counterparts on the desktop PC were given in Chapters Four and Five. In the example below, we will copy a rich-text format file on the desktop PC to the handheld PC, converting it to an appropriate format in the process.

1 On the desktop PC, open Windows Explorer and navigate to the folder which contains the file you want to copy to the handheld.

2 Make sure your handheld is turned on, then open HPC Explorer on the desktop PC and navigate to the folder on the handheld to which you want to copy the file.

Windows Explorer   HPC Explorer

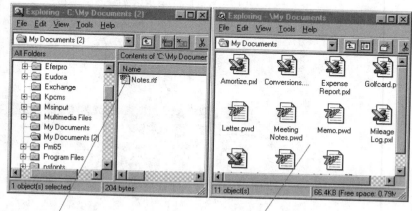

HANDY TIP **If you want to copy or move more than one file, hold down the Control (CTRL) key in step 3 as you click on each successive file.**

3 In Windows Explorer, click on the file you want to copy.

4 Drag the file over into the destination directory on the handheld.

HPC Explorer begins to copy and convert the file to the handheld format automatically:

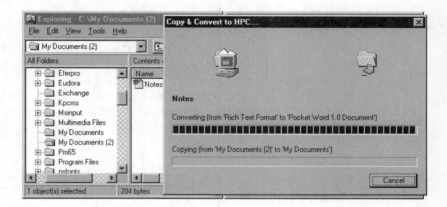

There is now a copy of the same file on both computers: Notes.rtf on the desktop PC, and Notes.pwd on the handheld.

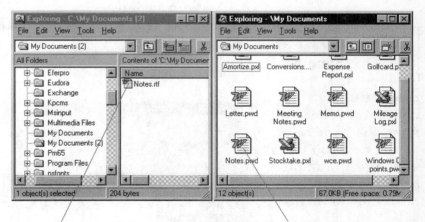

Original file on desktop PC   Copy on handheld PC

In this example, a file that is not application-specific has been converted to an application-specific file: *.pwd files are Pocket Word files. This is because Pocket Word is the only application on the handheld that can handle the formatting information in a rich-text format file. If you wish to change the default settings of which formats are used for file conversion, see the following topic.

Changing file-conversion properties

When you installed HPC Explorer, a list of defaults was automatically set regarding how files would be converted when being copied or moved between the desktop PC and the handheld. For example, Word files (*.doc) are converted into Pocket Word (*.pwd) format; Excel files (*.xls, *.xlb) into Pocket Excel (*.pxl) format; and Windows bitmap files (*.bmp) into special greyscale bitmap files (*.2bp).

If you are not satisfied with any of these defaults (for example, if there is a different format type which you feel would translate your file better), you can change them. Do the following:

I In HPC Explorer, open the Tools menu and select File Conversion.

The process of changing the properties for converting files from the handheld to the desktop PC is virtually the same as the method described here: just select the HPC > Desktop tab instead, in step 2.

2 To change the settings for how files on the desktop PC are converted to the handheld's format, select this tab.

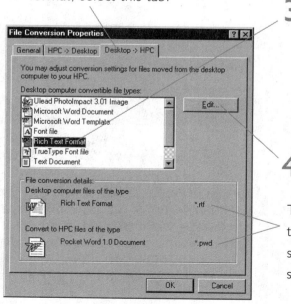

3 Select the desktop PC file type whose conversion settings you wish to change.

4 Click here.

The selected file type's current settings are shown here.

5 Click here to reveal a list of the file types to which the selected file type can be converted.

6 Select a file type from the list.

7 Click OK.

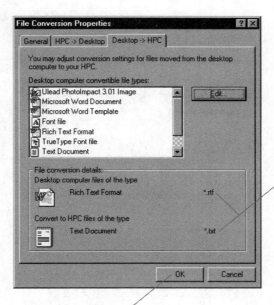

When you return to the File Conversion Properties window, the settings for the selected file type are changed.

8 Click OK to apply your changes.

Backing up handheld PC files

If, at a later date, you are happy with the settings made in step 3, you can select "Back Up Now" from the Tools menu. This takes you straight to step 5.

The first backup option, "Full", causes every file on your handheld to be backed up onto your desktop PC's hard drive, regardless of whether or not it has been backed up in the past. Choosing the second option, "Incremental", on the other hand, only backs up those files that have been created or amended since the last time you performed a backup. If this is your first backup, it makes little difference which type you choose.

When you back up the files on your desktop PC, you probably save the backup on floppy disks, or perhaps a Zip or Jaz drive. On your handheld this is not possible, since it doesn't have any internal or external drives. Therefore, when you want to back files up on the handheld, you save the files onto the hard drive of your desktop PC; these can then be saved or backed up from the desktop in the normal way. To do this, follow the steps below:

1 In HPC Explorer, open the Tools menu and select Backup/Restore.

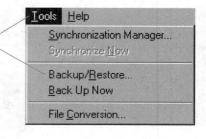

2 Make sure the Backup tab is selected.

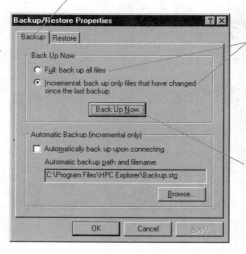

3 Select the type of backup you want to perform (see the Remember tip on the left).

4 Click on the "Back Up Now" button.

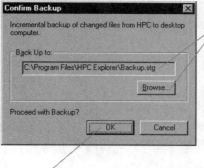

5 In this dialog box, you are asked to confirm that you want to perform the selected backup type. If you want to back up to another directory than the one shown here, click the Browse button.

6 Click OK.

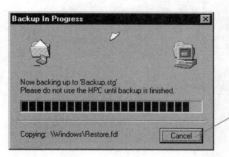

7 The backup starts. This usually takes around three or four minutes. If you want to cancel the operation, click here.

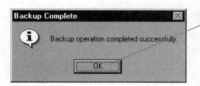

8 When the backup is complete, this message is displayed. Click here to return to the Backup/ Restore Properties window, then click OK again.

Restoring backed-up files

To restore backed-up files to their original locations on the handheld PC, use the following procedure:

1 In HPC Explorer, select Backup/Restore from the Tools menu.

2 Select the Restore tab.

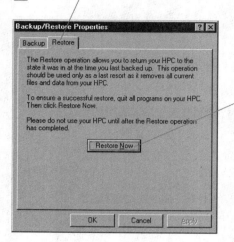

3 Click the Restore Now button.

4 If you want to restore a backup other than the one specified here, locate it by clicking the Browse button.

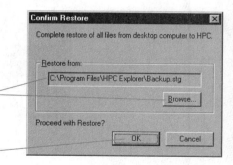

5 Click OK.

6 Take heed of this warning! If you wish to continue with the restore action and replace all the files currently on the handheld with the files in the backup, click here.

Internet Communications

By connecting your handheld PC to the Internet you gain access to a virtually limitless wealth of information in practically any field of interest you can imagine. This chapter begins by explaining how to set up an Internet connection. Next, it explains how to install Pocket Internet Explorer and use it to browse the web. Finally, the setup and use of Inbox, the email program, are explained.

Covers

Chapter Nine

Configuring a dial-up connection

Before you can connect your handheld PC to the Internet in order to browse the web or exchange email, you need to connect a modem card and then configure the Windows CE communications software. Once you have fitted the modem card according to the hardware manufacturer's instructions, configure the software as follows:

1 Select Programs from the Start menu.

2 Double-tap on the Communications icon.

3 Double-tap the Remote Networking shortcut icon.

4 Double-tap here.

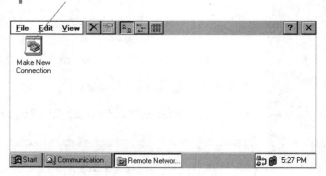

5 Enter a name for the connection.

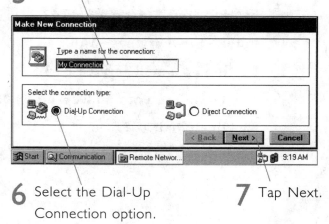

6 Select the Dial-Up Connection option.

7 Tap Next.

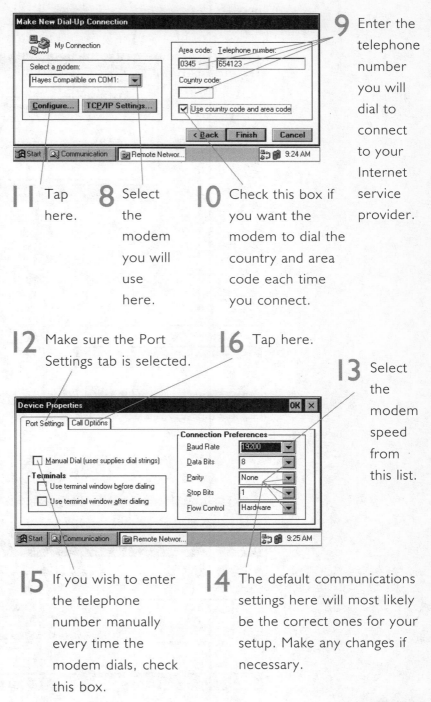

9 Enter the telephone number you will dial to connect to your Internet service provider.

11 Tap here.

8 Select the modem you will use here.

10 Check this box if you want the modem to dial the country and area code each time you connect.

12 Make sure the Port Settings tab is selected.

16 Tap here.

13 Select the modem speed from this list.

15 If you wish to enter the telephone number manually every time the modem dials, check this box.

14 The default communications settings here will most likely be the correct ones for your setup. Make any changes if necessary.

19 Tap OK to apply your changes.

18 Check this box if you don't want the modem to dial unless it detects the carrier tone.

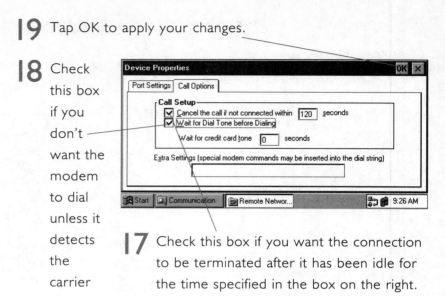

17 Check this box if you want the connection to be terminated after it has been idle for the time specified in the box on the right.

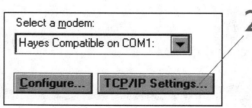

20 Back in the Make New Dial-Up Connection window, tap on the TCP/IP Settings button.

21 Most servers automatically assign you an IP address, as well as primary and secondary DNS addresses, when you dial up. However, if your service provider has specified that you should enter any of these addresses manually,

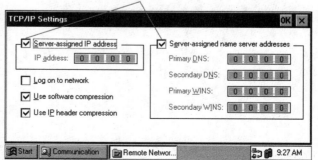

uncheck the appropriate box, then enter the address specified by the provider.

22 Tap the OK button in the TCP/IP Settings window, and then Finish in the Make New Dial-Up Connection window.

When you return to the view of the Remote Networking folder, you will see that an icon for your new connection now exists; see the topic below.

Connecting to the Internet

When you have configured the settings for your dial-up connection, you are almost ready to connect to the Internet. Do the following:

1 Double-tap on the icon that represents the connection you want to establish.

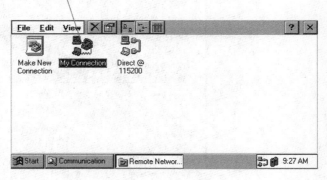

2 In the Connect To dialog box, enter the user name and password assigned to you by your service provider, then tap the Connect button.

Once your connection has been established, you should open the application you want to use. See the following topics for how to install and operate Pocket Internet Explorer and Inbox.

9 Internet Communications **135**

Installing Pocket Internet Explorer

When you installed HPC Explorer from the Windows CE CD-ROM, you were given the option to install the setup files for Pocket Internet Explorer onto the hard drive of your desktop PC. These setup files are then used to install Pocket Internet Explorer onto your handheld. If you did not install the setup files, follow the procedures below.

Installing the Pocket Internet Explorer setup files

To install the setup files, you need the Windows CE CD-ROM. Insert it into the desktop PC's CD-ROM drive. If AutoPlay is enabled on your PC, you should see the window below; if not, follow step 1:

> 1. Select "Run" from the Start menu. Click on the Browse button, and locate the CD-ROM drive, then run the file in its root directory called "Setup.exe" (the ".exe" extension may not be shown).

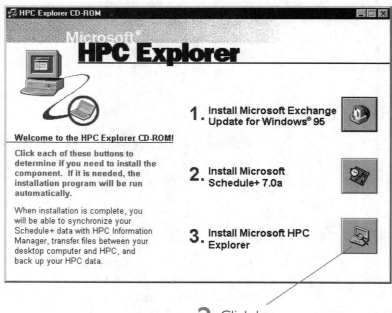

2 Click here.

3 Since you have
already set up HPC
Explorer, you are
offered the chance
to reinstall the same
files you did before
– i.e., excluding the
Pocket Internet
Explorer setup files. Click No.

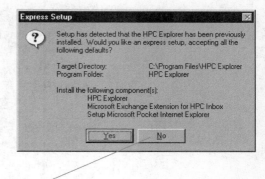

4 Fill in any requested information in the subsequent screens,
clicking the Next button until you get to the following screen:

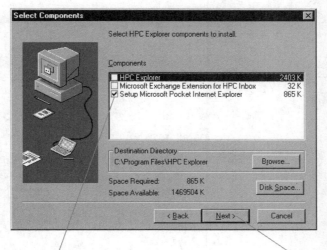

5 Uncheck all of the boxes here   6 Click Next.
except for the one labelled "Setup
Microsoft Pocket Internet Explorer".

7 Proceed through the following screens, then click Finish.

Setting up Pocket Internet Explorer on the handheld

Once you have installed the Pocket Internet Explorer setup files on the hard drive of your desktop PC, you are ready to install the program onto the handheld PC. Do the following:

1 From the Start menu, select Programs>HPC Explorer>Setup Microsoft Pocket Internet Explorer.

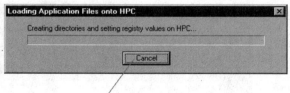

| HPC Explorer |
| HPC Explorer Release Notes |
| Setup Microsoft Pocket Internet Explorer |

2 Enter the information requested by the Setup Wizard, clicking on Next to proceed to each following screen.

Loading Application Files onto HPC

Creating directories and setting registry values on HPC...

[Cancel]

3 If you decide to cancel the setup process by clicking here, the installation will be incomplete, and you will have to run the setup program again before being able to run Pocket Internet Explorer.

Microsoft Pocket Internet Explorer

ⓘ Setup complete. To run Pocket IE double tap the Pocket IE icon on your HPC desktop.

[OK]

4 Click OK to close the Setup Wizard.

There should now be an icon for Pocket Internet Explorer on your handheld's main screen (see the following page).

Starting Pocket Internet Explorer

To start Pocket Explorer in order to browse the World-Wide Web, do the following:

| Double-tap on the Pocket IE icon.

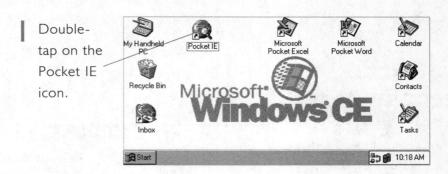

If the shortcut icon for Pocket Internet Explorer has been deleted from your handheld's main screen, select Programs> Communications> Pocket IE from the Start menu.

The main elements of the screen are pointed out below:

File, Edit, View, Favorites menus

Open Internet address

Open Favorites

Add to Favorites

Go to Start page

Search the web

Close Pocket IE

Help

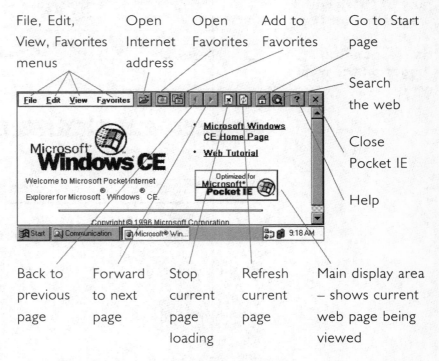

Back to previous page

Forward to next page

Stop current page loading

Refresh current page

Main display area – shows current web page being viewed

The page shown in Pocket IE's display area on startup is just a "dummy" page which resides on your handheld's memory storage. This will be replaced by any page you load subsequently from the web or elsewhere.

Browsing the web

To browse the World-Wide Web, do the following:

1 Open your Internet connection as described in the topic "Connecting to the Internet", earlier in this chapter.

2 Start Pocket IE, as described on the previous page.

 There are several web hyperlinks on Pocket IE's default startup screen. Tapping on any of these will cause Pocket IE to link to the corresponding pages on the web.

3 Tap here.

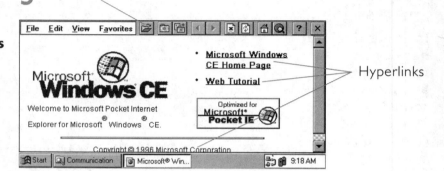

Hyperlinks

4 Enter a web address here.   5 Tap OK.

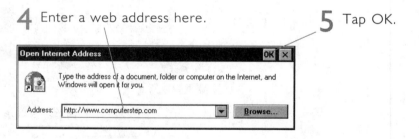

While the page is loading, you should see this animated symbol in the top right-hand corner of the main Pocket Internet Explorer window. You should normally wait while this symbol is displayed before attempting to read the page or follow its links.

...contd

If the page exists, it should be displayed after a short while in the main Pocket IE window:

Buttons like this, normally arranged across one edge of a web page, will almost certainly be hyperlinks to other web pages.

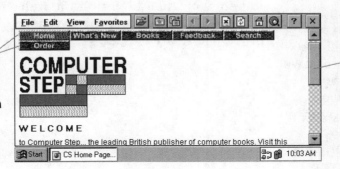

Drag the scrollbar up or down to view the rest of the page.

Following hyperlinks

In steps 3-5 on the previous page, a web page was opened by typing its address, or URL (Uniform Resource Locator), into the Open Internet Address dialog box. Once you have entered an initial URL like this, however, you will most likely move to other web pages by tapping on *hyperlinks*, which are web addresses embedded in text or images that appear on the screen.

If you see any underlined text on a web page, it is likely (though by no means certain) that that text is a hyperlink: tapping on it should jump to another page on the web. Graphical elements such as buttons or company logos can also act as hyperlinks.

In the desktop version of Internet Explorer, it is easy to tell which are hyperlinks: whenever you move your cursor over one, the cursor changes to a pointing hand symbol. Additionally, text hyperlinks usually appear in a different colour from the main body text. In Pocket IE, however, there is no such sure-fire way of determining which elements of the screen are hyperlinks; though it is usually quite clear (from the context, or textual invitations to "click here") which are links. Trial and error is usually your best policy.

...contd

 The "Move
to next
page"
button
cannot anticipate
which page follows
any given page,
since most web
pages link to more
than one other
page. Rather, this
button lets you
move forward
through the pages
once again, after
you have reviewed
pages using the
"Move to previous
page" button.

Using the navigation buttons

Pocket IE provides a number of buttons which are designed
to help you when browsing the web, freeing you from
relying solely on hyperlinks to move from one page to the
other. These are as follows:

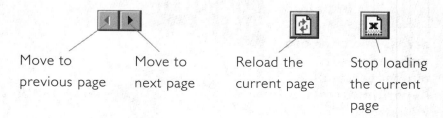

Move to   Move to   Reload the   Stop loading
previous page   next page   current page   the current
                                                       page

Adding URLs to the Favorites folder

After you have spent some time browsing the web, you are
likely to have found some pages to which you would like to
return regularly. To do this, you don't have to remember
their URLs, or write them down on a scrap of paper: it's
much more convenient to add them to the Favorites folder.
This a folder located in the Windows directory, in which
Pocket IE saves one file (with the extension *.url) for every
location you mark as a favourite. To add an entry to the
Favorites folder, do the following:

1 Open the page you want to save as a favourite.

2 Open the Favorites menu and tap on the "Add to Favorites"
entry, or tap on this button.

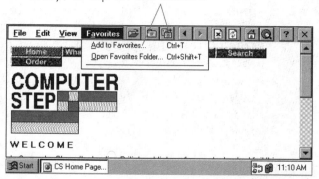

The Add to Favorites dialog box appears:

3 If the default name is acceptable, leave this box as it is; otherwise, enter a better name here.

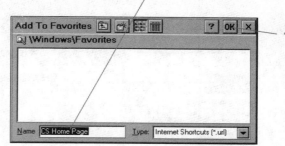

4 Tap OK to add the URL to the Favorites folder.

Creating subfolders within the Favorites folder

If you add many URLs to the Favorites folder using only the method shown on the previous page, you will soon end up with a very long, confusing list; you need some way of organising it. Thankfully, you can create folders within the Favorites folder, so that URLs can be saved according to category, or whatever other criteria you wish. To create a new folder when saving a URL, do the following:

1 Follow steps 1 and 2 on the previous page to open the Add to Favorites dialog box.

REMEMBER

The Favorites folder is just like any other folder on your handheld. You can create any number of subfolders within a folder, allowing for many levels of subcategorisation. Also, you can edit the contents of the Favorites folder using Windows CE Explorer.

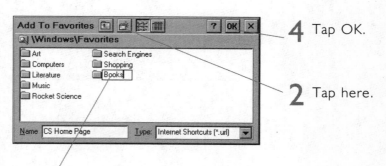

4 Tap OK.

2 Tap here.

3 A new subfolder is created. Enter a name for it.

5 The new folder is opened. Amend the name of the URL if necessary, then tap OK.

Opening URLs in the Favorites folder

Once you have saved a URL in the Favorites folder, opening it is a very easy process. Do the following:

1. Open the Favorites menu and select a favourite from the list of recently opened favourites at the bottom of the menu; or...

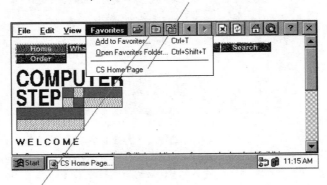

2. If the favourite you are looking for is not listed at the bottom of the menu, select "Open Favorites Folder" from the Favorites menu, or tap on this button.

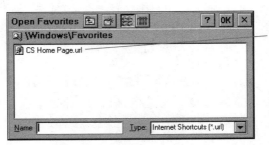

3. Double-tap on the favourite you want to open.

Speeding up your web browsing

If you are using your handheld PC to browse the web, the chances are that you have done the same with your desktop PC. Even with such a comparatively powerful processor as that, the speed at which web pages are loaded can often be grindingly slow, because of busy web servers or slow connections. On your handheld PC, you are likely to experience even slower loading times, because of the hardware restrictions of the machine itself.

One way to speed up the rate at which web pages load, on any computer, is to tell your browser not to load the elements which form the biggest files, and hence which always take the longest to download: pictures and sounds. To do this, use the following steps.

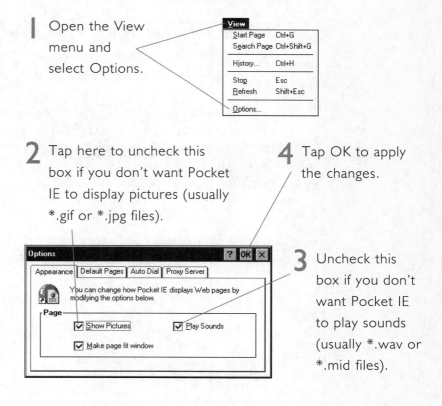

1 Open the View menu and select Options.

View	
Start Page	Ctrl+G
Search Page	Ctrl+Shift+G
History...	Ctrl+H
Stop	Esc
Refresh	Shift+Esc
Options...	

2 Tap here to uncheck this box if you don't want Pocket IE to display pictures (usually *.gif or *.jpg files).

4 Tap OK to apply the changes.

3 Uncheck this box if you don't want Pocket IE to play sounds (usually *.wav or *.mid files).

Options ? OK ×

Appearance | Default Pages | Auto Dial | Proxy Server

You can change how Pocket IE displays Web pages by modifying the options below.

Page
- ☑ Show Pictures   ☑ Play Sounds
- ☑ Make page fit window

...contd

Any pages you load subsequently will not have their pictures displayed or their sounds played; in place of each image, a blank frame marked with a ⊞ icon will appear, as below:

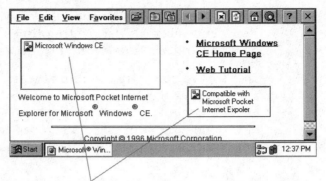

These frames mark the places of images which are not displayed. Many frames will contain text which explains the nature of the image.

If you decide, after loading a web page with text only, that you do want to view its images, repeat steps 1, 2 and 4 on the previous page to check the Show Pictures box. Next, tap on the Refresh button to view the page with the new settings applied.

Setting your Start page

Every time Pocket Internet Explorer loads, it displays a page known as the Start page. By default, this is the page shown at the beginning of the "Browsing the web" topic – a Windows CE page located in your handheld's storage memory which contains some links to related Microsoft sites. You are not restricted to using this as your Start page; you might want to start with your service provider's web page, or even your own home page on the web. To change the URL that Pocket IE searches for on startup, do the following:

1 Open the local or remote web page that you want to be your new Start page.

You can also use the Defaults tab to change the URL of the search engine that is accessed when you tap on the Search button. Open the search engine that you want to use, then follow steps 1-3 on this page. Next, tap here and select Search Page from the list; then follow steps 4 and 5.

2 Open the View menu and select Options.

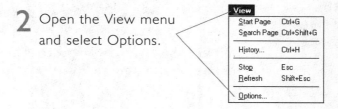

3 Select the Default Pages tab.

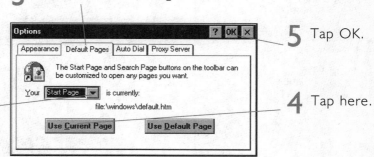

5 Tap OK.

4 Tap here.

Opening the Start and Search pages quickly

You can jump to your Start page or Search page at any time by tapping on these buttons in the Pocket IE toolbar:

Start page

Search page

Inbox – an overview

Inbox is the application you use to manage your email on your handheld. In this respect, it is roughly equivalent to Exchange or Internet Mail on your desktop PC. You can use it to read email, compose email, and swap messages with Exchange on the desktop. To open inbox, do the following:

Double-tap on this icon.

The main Inbox window appears. The main elements of the screen are pointed out below:

File, Compose, Service menus

New message

Reply to sender

Reply to all recipients

Forward message

Mail categories – tap on an icon to view the contents of that folder

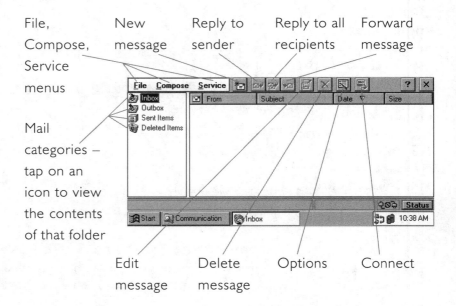

Edit message

Delete message

Options

Connect

Setting up a mail service

Before Inbox can start handling your mail, you need to set up a mail service; i.e., give Inbox some details about your Internet connection and the mail server which handles all of your email. To do this, follow the steps below:

Tap on the Options icon in the Inbox toolbar.

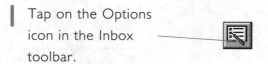

The Options dialog box appears:

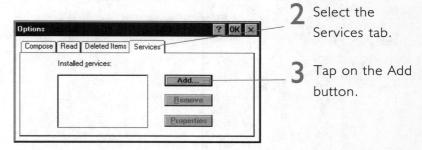

2 Select the Services tab.

3 Tap on the Add button.

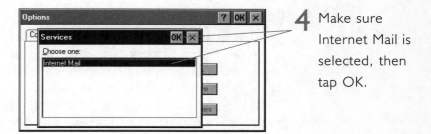

4 Make sure Internet Mail is selected, then tap OK.

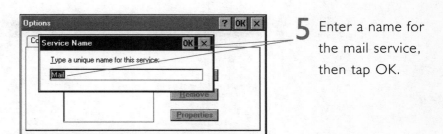

5 Enter a name for the mail service, then tap OK.

6 Tap here and select the Internet connection you wish to use.

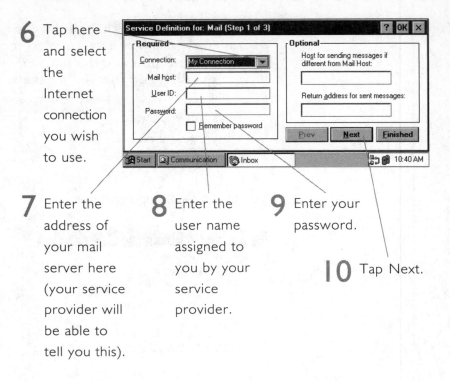

7 Enter the address of your mail server here (your service provider will be able to tell you this).

8 Enter the user name assigned to you by your service provider.

9 Enter your password.

10 Tap Next.

In the dialog box which follows, you can probably leave most of the options with their default values. The Address Book section of this dialog allows you to select which field of your Contacts database the email addresses should be imported from. This means that if you have already entered all of your contacts' email addresses into the Contacts application (see Chapter Six), you don't have to re-enter them for Inbox.

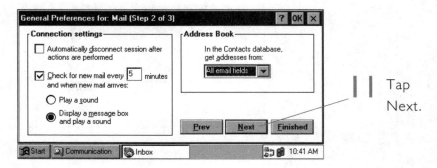

11 Tap Next.

The final dialog box allows you to specify how Inbox downloads your mail. Perform step 12 and/or 13, then step 14.

12 Tap here if you only want to download the message headers

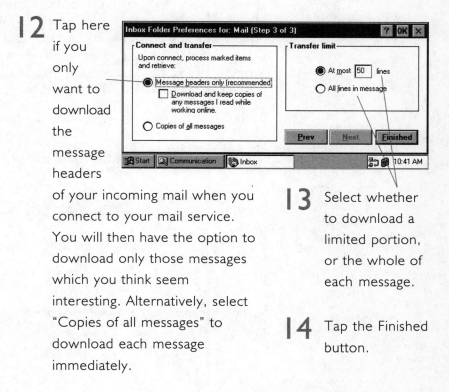

of your incoming mail when you connect to your mail service. You will then have the option to download only those messages which you think seem interesting. Alternatively, select "Copies of all messages" to download each message immediately.

13 Select whether to download a limited portion, or the whole of each message.

14 Tap the Finished button.

Connecting to your mail service

Once you have entered the details of your mail service, you can connect to it. When you do this, a number of things happen. First, Inbox checks to see whether you have been sent any new mail, and downloads the headers (and the messages, if you specified that this should happen). Next, it downloads the contents of any messages whose headers you selected for download the last time you checked your mail. Finally, Inbox sends any outgoing mail that you have composed and placed in your outbox.

To connect to your mail service, do the following:

1 Tap the Connect button in the Inbox toolbar.

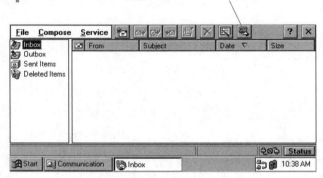

2 In the Connect To dialog box, enter your user name, password and (optionally) domain name, if these have not been saved from a previous connection.

3 Tap the Connect button.

Reading email

Once you have connected to your mail service to download some messages and/or headers, you will see some entries in the main message list. You should normally disconnect then, so that you are not wasting your telephone bill while you read any messages you have downloaded, and decide which new messages to download in full.

If you look at your Inbox folder, you will see that some of the message headers are in **bold** type, while others are plain. The bold messages are those that you have not yet read; when you read them, their headers change to plain text.

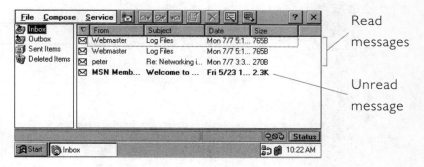

Read messages

Unread message

REMEMBER

Re step 1 – the number of lines downloaded was specified in step 13 of "Setting up a mail service".

Marking a message for download

1 To download only a portion of a message, double-tap the message's header to mark it with the 📄 icon; or...

2 To download all of a message, select its header, then choose "Retrieve Full Text Copy" from the Service menu.

3 The next time you connect to the mail service, the message is downloaded. Follow the steps below to read the message.

Reading a downloaded message

1 Double-tap on its header in the message list.

2 If you want to reply to the message, tap on the 📧 button, then see the following page.

Composing email

To compose a new email message, you may want to reply directly to an email that has been sent to you; to do this, follow step 2 on the previous page. However, to send a new message that is unrelated to any email you have received, do the following:

1 Tap on the [button] button in the main Inbox toolbar.

2 Make sure that To: is selected in the drop-down list, then enter the email address of the recipient here.

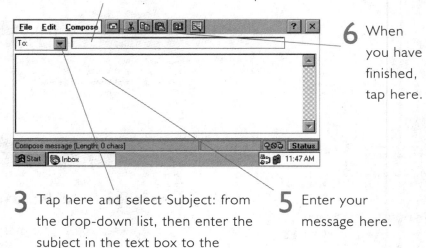

6 When you have finished, tap here.

3 Tap here and select Subject: from the drop-down list, then enter the subject in the text box to the right.

5 Enter your message here.

4 Select any other fields from the drop-down list, then enter the appropriate text in the text box.

After step 6, if you are working off-line at the moment, then the message is placed in your Outbox; the next time you connect to your mail server, the message will be sent. However, if you are currently connected to the mail server, then it is sent immediately.

Index